Spiritual Things

Exploring our Connection to God, the Angels, and the Heavenly Realm

Brian M. Rossiter

I would like to thank my dear friend John Pierce for his help in putting this book into its finished form.

All Bible references are taken from the NASB, unless otherwise noted. Cover art by Geraldine Dukes.

Table of Contents

Preface

When I was an early teenager—probably about thirteen or fourteen years old—my father told me about my great-grandmother's passing. He was there in those final hours, as she drifted away from the world of the living. Though I never met my great-grandmother, I have always heard that she was a woman of tremendous faith. Like so many others, she struggled mightily throughout the days leading up to her death. It was during one of those final days that my father suddenly knew he needed to change his plans and drive over to be by her side. For reasons no one can explain, he knew he had to go *right then*. As expected, the old woman was exceedingly close to "her time" upon his arrival. The mysterious part of the whole thing was her actions just before she passed. With the last of her strength and her final breaths, she reached toward the sky, in an effort to touch something that was only visible to her. To this day, I wonder: what did she see? What was it that gave her such peace in her time of ultimate trial? "Grandma Martha" departed almost immediately after, but not without the comfort of whatever heavenly reality she had seen.

Personally, I believe my grandmother was reaching into "the heavens." By that, I do not mean "into the sky." Rather, she was reaching into a realm of existence that we are simply unable to see or experience most of the time. Maybe she saw an angel. Maybe she saw a vision of someone familiar to her. Maybe she saw Christ himself. I really don't know. Nevertheless, I am sure she saw *something* that was real. More likely, she saw *someone* who is real. These types of subjects force us to ponder a multitude of issues. Have you ever wondered what God does with His time? What about the angels: what are they up to on a daily basis? What are they all doing right now, at this very moment? What does it mean to be made "in the image of God," and to be "a little lower than the angels"? The truth is that most of us have never really given any of these questions much thought or attention. I will openly confess that, up until the last several years, I had personally never investigated them in great detail.

When you think about it, this is a rather strange phenomenon. The Bible contains quite a lot of information about God, the angels, and the ways in which they interact with us. More than that, it provides a vision of what we should expect our existence to ultimately look like. Certainly, we are not given a full glimpse into every aspect of these realities, as some of the biblical authors were. But if we add a bit of thought and imagination to the biblical information, we may yet be able to see the bigger picture. More than understanding the many ways that heaven and earth intersect, we can begin to see where the two are heading: where *we* are heading. Within the church, talk of "spiritual things" like these are at least as common now as they ever have been: perhaps even more so. Even within the secular world, there is a significant interest in spiritism, what role the dead might play in our world, and many other related topics. Despite this obvious enthusiasm, we seldom ask the most fundamental questions. What does it mean to be "spiritual?" What is heaven like? How do we interact with the entities who live there, and what similarities do we share with them? This book is about understanding the nature of the heavenly beings, and our relationship with them both at the present and in the future. Further, it is about understanding how drastically these matters affect our lives. To put it simply, this book is about "spiritual things."

Chapter One

Physical Beings

In all of life, there may not be a more important (and enigmatic) question than this: what does it mean to be made in the "image of God?" Does this have to do with our interior qualities, our physical appearances, or perhaps some blend of both? Closely associated to these questions, we must also ask about our connection to the other created beings: the angels. In what ways do we resemble them, and what influence do they have on our lives? To better comprehend humanity and our role in existence, we must first begin by taking a hard look at how the Bible describes those who are superior to us. By seeing a clearer picture of who God and the angels are, we will also see a much clearer picture of who we are. If we truly are made in the image of God, we must understand who God is in order to make sense of this reality.

Throughout history, much has been written and taught concerning how we should view our Creator. The interesting thing is that a great deal of it does not align with what the biblical texts tell us. When one seeks to understand these matters through the lens of Scripture—and not chiefly through philosophy, science, or some other epistemology—a view emerges that many of us would not recognize. While we have been trained to believe that everything having to do with "spiritual things" is different than our world and is typically non-physical, this may not actually be the case. In fact, many of the ways in which the biblical authors described God, the angels, and the heavenly world is, *at times*, leagues apart from what is advocated in churches and universities around the globe. It is the latter of these three topics that I will discuss first. In a sense, our beliefs about heaven have bearing on almost every other aspect of this book. This is most certainly true with regards to how we view God and the angels. With that knowledge in place, we will be prepared to launch into a full-scale investigation of the incredible entities who live in heaven.

Heaven is a Realm

History is replete with images of God and the heavenly host sitting on clouds and floating around in the sky. Though there is a small degree of truth represented in these concepts, this is far from a complete picture of things. Before we delve into some of the other fascinating topics we will examine, it is absolutely critical that we understand one very important concept: *heaven is a realm of existence.* Heaven is not literally "above us"—though, as I will explain, there is a connection there—nor does it exist in the distant recesses of space. When evaluating this issue from a biblical perspective, nearly every piece of evidence concerning the heavenly abode suggests that it is not contained within our universe. Instead, heaven is another world that is going on right alongside of our own. It is typically hidden from our sight but is unmistakably real. We might think of heaven as an invisible layer that rests overtop earth: a wholly separate location that still has significant bearing on our own world. While I believe that viewing the habitation of both God and the angels as a realm of its own seems unavoidable, I realize this is probably a completely foreign concept to many of us. Since this belief is so thoroughly foundational to my overall position throughout this book (and any other), I feel that I must spend some time elaborating on this concept up front.

I could make this very easy and point out the philosophical problems with believing that God—and therefore, heaven too—is contained within the known universe or that He lives in the sky. Consider this: if God created the universe, how could He exist within it? Obviously, God could not be confined within something that He would *later* bring into existence; no matter how you look at it, that would be impossible.[1]

For comparison, workers could not create a building if they were standing inside of it. Technicians could not build a car if they were already sitting within it. A bird could not make a nest if it were already living in that nest. In all of these cases, the agent creating the object would have to exist outside of it. While that point would be sufficient on its own, we have a wealth of other reasons why we can be certain that heaven is a different realm of existence. In particular, the Bible itself gives us plenty of reasons to believe this.

For starters, consider when Elisha and his servant were surrounded by an entire army of Aramean soldiers. Though the servant was extremely alarmed by the situation, Elisha was not. 2 Kings 6:16-17 records Elisha's response to his servant and the events that followed:

> "So he answered, 'Do not fear, for those who are with us are more than those who are with them.' Then Elisha prayed and said, 'O Lord, I pray, open his eyes that he may see.' And the Lord opened the servant's eyes and he saw; and behold, the mountain was full of horses and chariots of fire all around Elisha."

This is one of the amazing moments within Scripture where we get a peek into the workings of the heavenly realm. It's almost as if God peeled back the curtain that prevents us mortals from seeing into that world, and allowed Elisha's servant to see the full scope and magnitude of all existence. The angelic beings (and their chariots) he saw certainly weren't from somewhere in outer space; they appeared in an instant. They were present with both him and Elisha the entire time, but they were veiled within the heavenly realm.

If something of this sort sounds familiar, it is because it also happened at our Lord's birth. Right after the birth of Christ, a group of

---

[1] This would be true in both the *ex nihilo* (creation "from nothing") and the *ex materia* (creation from pre-existing matter) views. Either way, God cannot be bound within something He has not yet created!

shepherds received quite a fright. While they were out in a nearby field, it is recorded that an angel ". . . suddenly stood before them, and the glory of the Lord shone around them; and they were terribly frightened" (Lk. 2:9). This is another case where, seemingly out of nowhere, an angel appeared. Furthermore, these very same shepherds would see more astonishing things thereafter. Luke 2:12-14 records the following:

> "This will be a sign for you: you will find a baby wrapped in cloths and lying in a manger.' And suddenly there appeared with the angel a multitude of the heavenly host praising God and saying, 'Glory to God in the highest, And on earth peace among men with whom He is pleased.' "

Notice the abrupt and unexpected nature of these events. In fact, the word used specifically in 2:13—which is *exaiphnés*—most specifically translates as either "suddenly" or "unexpectedly."[2]

This event was by no means the only time when the two realms become obvious. In the book of Ephesians, the apostle Paul literally referred to the existence of the heavenly realm on multiple occasions. In all, he mentioned this sphere of existence five times in the letter alone.[3] Though the word Paul used here (*epouranios*) directly translates to "heavenly" or "celestial," it clearly implies something of a realm or a sphere of existence. The term intensifies the more common word *ouranos*, which means "heaven." The word is used in Ephesians (and elsewhere) to contrast beings or features of the earthly realm with beings or features of the heavenly realm. In 1 Corinthians, Paul even uses *epouranios* to compare the type of bodies we have now to the type possessed by the heavenly beings (15:48-49). That particular issue will be extremely important at other points in this book.

As if this information were not enough to prove that God and the angels inhabit another realm and do not live somewhere in space, we have

---

[2] Strong's Concordance, 1810.
[3] See 1:3, 1:20, 2:6, 3:10, and 6:12.

the resurrection appearances of Jesus to consider. Jesus showed himself to his disciples, and many others, time and time again after the Resurrection. He appeared to Mary Magdalene outside of the tomb just after he rose from the dead (Jn. 20:15). He appeared to the horrified apostles on two separate occasions—with more than a week between the visitations—as they huddled behind a locked door (Jn. 20:19, 26). Prior to that, Jesus met the apostles while they were out fishing in the Sea of Tiberias (Jn. 21:1). He also appeared to more than five hundred people at the same time (1 Cor. 15:6). My personal favorite appearance of Jesus was on the road to Emmaus, where he walked and talked with two of his disciples for the duration of the seven-mile journey from Jerusalem to Emmaus (Lk. 24:13-35). Perhaps more astonishing than the fact that the disciples never understood who he was until they ate dinner that evening is that Jesus pulled the greatest Houdini act ever conceived by mankind in their presence. Right after Jesus blessed the meal, and the disciples *finally* began to understand the strange man's identity, the Gospel of Luke records that Jesus proceeded to "vanish from their sight" (Lk. 24:31). Here, Jesus did not utilize trap doors, magic curtains, smokescreens, or anything of the sort. Rather, he had completely disappeared; he was there, and then he was gone.

The question that must be asked with regards to these appearances (and disappearances) is obvious: where was Jesus the rest of the time? When he wasn't eating, drinking, speaking, and even being touched (Thomas touched his side), what was Jesus doing, and where was he doing it? Notice that there is not a single verse in the Bible having to do with the post-Resurrection appearances that mentions how Jesus left the scene. Barring the all-so-pivotal Ascension—where Jesus both literally and symbolically departed "back to heaven" for the final time (Acts 1:6-11)—there is no record of how Jesus flew off into the atmosphere, slipped away and hid inside of a house, or how he simply wandered away from those around him. Just as he had done after walking on the road to Emmaus, Jesus seems to have been able to utterly vanish from human view at will.

Unlike Frodo Baggins in *The Lord of the Rings* trilogy, Jesus didn't need a ring to depart from our sight; he had a perfectly good resurrection body for that.

As we progress through other topics, you will see additional reasons to believe that heaven is a realm. As I said earlier, this reality affects—in one way or another—almost every other aspect of this book. However, these examples should suffice to show that there is both a biblical and logical precedent for this view. More than that, it should already be apparent that thinking of heaven as being "up there" or believing that God exists in the sky is not accurate. With a clearer understanding of heaven in place, we are prepared to discuss the beings that live within it.

Lost Images

Welcome to Sunday school 101; human beings were made in the image of God. Obviously, this does not come as a surprise to anyone. The problem is that the vast majority of people who claim to believe this do not fully. Sure, we are somehow "like" God, but that statement comes with more than a few caveats. Every time this enigmatic statement has come up in my presence—whether that be at a church, a classroom, or elsewhere—I have heard the same general commentary on the issue. While most people do not tend to go into detail, there is almost always a local leader or theologian who is eager to clear it up for everyone. Typically, their explanations go something like this: "We are image-bearers, which means that we are in many respects like God. We are rational beings who think. We are personal agents. We love, and we have relationships. We experience a plethora of emotions and feelings. Yes, we are like God . . . *but this has nothing to do with physical appearances.*" Indeed—this has nothing to do with appearances. That is the standard narrative.

Though I probably do not need to provide many examples of this type of thinking, because most of us have heard something of the sort before, I want to provide a few to show my point. The first comes from the extremely prominent medieval Sephardic philosopher, Maimonides. In his third of the Thirteen Principles of Faith, he left no doubt about what Jewish followers should believe about God:

> "I believe by complete faith that the Creator, blessed be His name, is not a body, is not affected by physical matter, and nothing whatsoever can compare to Him [or be compared with Him]."[4]

While this view was out of step with many of his contemporaries, Maimonides would have found himself in good company among most Christian thinkers of the time. Speaking of Christian thinkers, the respected Scottish theologian, James Orr, once summarized the way in which we bear God's image as follows:

> "It lies in the nature of the case that the 'image' does not consist in bodily form; it can only reside in spiritual qualities, in man's mental and moral attributes as a self-conscious, rational, personal agent, capable of self-determination and obedience to moral law."[5]

Certainly, this assessment is quite true in many respects. It is well articulated and meaningful. Existing in God's image does have much to do with "spiritual qualities," mental and moral attributes, rationality, agency, self-determination, and obedience. I have no qualms with those descriptions, and I would doubt that most Christians do. Of course, there is still the matter of the first line of his statement.

I recently came across another, more contemporary, example while reading Dr. Glenn Sunshine's book, *The Image of God*. At the onset of the book—before making the positive case—he discusses what being made in the image of God does *not* mean. As you can imagine, the issue of God's corporeality is among the first on the list:

---

4 See "Maimonides' 13 Principles of Jewish Faith."
5 James Orr, "God, Image Of."

"The image of God is not found in human beings having a body like God's . . . Scripture is clear that God is Spirit (Jn. 4:24) and the only body He has is Jesus'. This is why the second commandment bans the use of images in worship: by their very nature no image can convey the essence of an invisible, non-corporeal being. Images thus conceal more than they reveal and they encourage us to think of God as less than and other than what He has revealed Himself to be."[6]

Though I will discuss John 4:24 in due time, it is worth mentioning now that this text is nearly always used as the key piece of evidence that God is incorporeal. Sunshine's appropriation of the second commandment is highly questionable, particularly because man was made in God's image to begin with. If images "conceal more than they reveal"—and are, thus, a negative thing—why would God create other beings in His *image*? Setting that aside, this is a clear example where all tangible associations between God and man are dismissed at the onset of the conversation. There just isn't a connection there; case closed.

We should find it curious that this issue is thought to be "settled" within the church. In reality, it never has been. David Clossen—writing on behalf of the ERLC of the Southern Baptist Convention—summarized this ambiguity clearly:

"Although 'image of God' has become ubiquitous in Christian literature and conversation in recent years, it has not been robustly defined. Perhaps this is due to the lack of agreement throughout church history on what exactly constitutes the image of God, which no doubt stems from the fact that Scripture declares but does not elaborate on the axiom in detail."[7]

---

[6] Glenn Sunshine, *The Image of* God, Loc. 104-116 (Kindle Version).

[7] ERLC stands for the "Ethics and Religious Liberty Commission." See the article, "What does it mean to be made in God's image."

As I will show, it is false that Scripture provides little detail on the matter. However, he is correct in saying that the "image of God" is not robustly defined and has not actually been agreed upon throughout church history. Biblical scholar, D.J.A. Clines, put the issue this way:

> "It appears that scholarship has reached something of an impasse over the problem of the image, in that different starting-points, all of which seem to be legitimate, lead to different conclusions. If one begins from the philological evidence, the image is defined in physical terms. If we begin from the incorporeality of God, the image cannot include the body of man. If we begin with the Hebrew conception of man's nature as a unity, we cannot separate, in such a fundamental sentence about man, the spiritual part of man from the physical. If we begin with 'male and female' as a definitive explanation of the image, the image can only be understood in terms of personal relationships, and the image of God must be located in mankind (or married couples!) rather than the individual man."[8]

With this in mind, I have to wonder why people have tended to believe that "God's image" should refer only to non-physical qualities. Who ever said that is the way we should view this whole issue? On whose authority does this belief rest? Is there a particular biblical text that demands this: some mandate that dictates our interpretation? I once simply assumed that there must be. I was taught that God *has to be* understood as an immaterial, unembodied being at both college and seminary, after all. I have read a lot of truly distinguished scholars who have said the same thing. This is why some have noted that Christian theologians have historically relied more on extra-biblical philosophical and theological sources than the biblical texts themselves.[9] As I will suggest throughout the book, this has led to the denigration of the physical body and a more dualistic understanding

---

[8] D.J.A Clines, "Tyndale Bulletin 19" (53-103).
[9] A very useful source on this matter is Richard Middleton's, *The Liberating Image*.

of the image of God within mainstream Christian theology. As is often the case, my view shifted on this matter when I finally took the time to research it for myself. There are really a number of reasons why I feel that we should question the idea that bearing God's image is an entirely immaterial issue. But first things first: what does the Bible actually say about this?

There are quite a number of terms that are associated—in some way, shape, or form—with the image discussion throughout the Bible. It only seems fitting that we should begin with the central term itself: the word "image." The Hebrew term *tselem* is what we primarily translate as the word image, and it (or one of its variants) is used seventeen times throughout the Old Testament.[10] Honest scholars have long pointed out that, as the biblical authors would have understood things, this term carried both a spiritual and a physical aspect to it.[11] Most notably, *tselem* is used very early on in the book of Genesis, when it describes the creation of our world. It is here that we are first told about our true identity: where we are told that a being greater than ourselves made us. Perhaps more amazingly, we are also told that we somehow resemble this being; "God said, let us make man in our image . . ." (1:26a). Naturally, there is more to the statement, but we will get to that. Certainly, this is a major declaration. What should we make of this: being made in God's image? To thoroughly answer that question, we need to investigate both where and how it is used elsewhere.

It may come as a surprise to some, as it first did to me, that the word *tselem* (image) is most often used to describe something that *physically* resembles something else. It is used to compare idols that have been fashioned in the image of some false deity (2 Ki. 11:18), like the well-known god Baal (2 Chr. 23:17). These were made to look exactly like how they perceived the gods to look. When the Philistines were considering returning the Ark of the Covenant to Israel, they wondered what kind of guilt offering they should return along with it. They found it fitting to send

---

[10] Strong's Concordance, "tselem."

[11] For a good example, see John Day's *From Creation to Babel*, page 14 in particular.

five gold tumors and five gold rats, since those plagues had struck them after taking the Ark (1 Sam. 6:4). Subsequently, they were told to make models ("images") of the tumors and rats, in an effort to avoid being punished by Yahweh (6:5). The tumors should look like tumors, and the rats like rats. In a much more obvious way, the book of Ezekiel describes how God's people saw pictures of the Chaldeans on a wall and began to lust after these images (23:14-16). The word "images" used in that reference pertained to exact replicas of living people; the pictures looked just like the Chaldean people. They were essentially portraits.

Clearly, *tselem* is used to describe several different relationships, but it is not the only term that is used to compare such things. The Hebrew *demuth* is what we typically translate as "likeness" within the Old Testament, where it is used twenty-five times. Generally, *demuth* translates as "likeness" or "similitude." In my way of thinking, this term means "to very strongly resemble" someone or something. As with *tselem*, *demuth* is used primarily to make tangible comparisons. King Ahaz once had an altar built that bared the same likeness as one that was built by the Assyrian king, Tiglath-Pilesar (2 Ki. 16:10-16). Ahaz, or his men, looked at the Assyrian altar and copied the blueprint. The Jewish people constructed items in the same likeness of cattle that served as temple furnishings (2 Chr. 4:3). The people looked at cattle and created precise models of them. These types of comparisons may have had something to do with the function of the objects being described, but there can be no doubt that the "likeness" described in these instances had something to do with literal appearances. They weren't comparing statues to cattle because they grunted or chewed their cud; they compared the two because they looked the same.

The most significant way that *demuth* is used, however, is when it compares us with God. Genesis tells us on more than one occasion that we were made in the "likeness" of God. The first reference is in 1:26, which was previously quoted. The second reference is often overlooked, but it may be more significant than most of us realize. The early portion of Genesis 5 recounts God's creative act of making Adam. First, it is restated that God created Adam in His own "likeness." We all knew that much. However, the statement made just two verses later is literally mind-blowing. Genesis 5:3 records the following: "When Adam had lived 130 years, he had a son *in his own likeness*, in *his own image*, and he named him Seth (emphasis, mine)." Did you notice what just happened there? Seth is being compared to Adam with *exactly* the same descriptive language that is used to compare Adam with God. In other words, Adam was like God just as Seth was like Adam. The actual language of the Old Testament tells us that we are similar to God in the same ways that our children are similar to us. Our sons and daughters are born in our likeness, and we were made in God's likeness.

The words "image" (*tselem*) and "likeness" (*demuth*) appear to be words that comprehensively compare one thing with another. Though some thinkers have considered the two to be quite different in function, the most natural understanding of these terms is in a complementary way; both stress the similarities that certain beings or items share with others. Now, please don't misunderstand me—I am not saying that either of these words discuss items or agents that are identical in all ways. We are not exactly like God in any way, shape, or form. We have not His power, His intelligence, His compassion, His creative ability, His wisdom, or anything else, in even close to equal measure. That being said, we should not underestimate the importance of these terms, either. Though neither one tells us that we are exactly like our Creator, both terms reveal that we are very, *very* much like Him. We have some measure of His power, His intelligence, His compassion, His creative ability, His wisdom, and a variety of other features. Perhaps we also possess some measure of God's physical appearance.

This may well be true when we look at the Old Testament descriptions, but surely the New Testament defines our similarities with God differently. Those texts will urge us to view the "image" and the "likeness" exclusively in terms of immaterial attributes and characteristics, right? To provide an answer to that question, we will need to thoughtfully evaluate the Greek terms that parallel the Hebrew words we previously examined. As we saw with *tselem* and *demuth*, there are basically two Greek terms that are of primary interest to us here: *eikón* and *homoióma*.

Let's take these terms in order, beginning with *eikón*. The word *eikón* is what we primarily translate as "image," so it is essentially the Greek equivalent of the Hebrew *tselem*. In all, either it or its variants are used twenty-three times throughout the New Testament. To me, it is not really the number of usages that is noteworthy; the ways in which the term is used is much more telling. For example, Jesus used the word *eikón* when he was asked whether he and his fellow Jews should pay taxes to Caesar. The question was a reasonably loaded one, being that it had become the practice of Roman emperors in those days to demand worship as a deity. In some sense, it could be thought that paying money to Caesar was the same as paying him homage as a god. Famously, Jesus took the coin and, looking at the "image" of Caesar imprinted on it, told his questioners to "render to Caesar the things that are Caesar's; and to God the things that are God's."[12] Right away, we see the power of the term. The image on the coin was a replica of the emperor. The picture physically looked like Tiberius Caesar. In the same vein, the word *eidolón*—which is from the same root word as *eikón*—is used to discuss idols throughout the New Testament. It, too, is used to describe the items crafted to physically resemble the false gods of the Greco-Roman world.

The word *eikón* is also used in some of the most powerful statements about Jesus' divinity in all the Bible. In Colossians 1:15, Paul told his fellow believers that Jesus is the "image of the invisible God." Paul made a strikingly similar statement in 2 Corinthians 4:4, where he revealed that Jesus is the "image of God." The idea that God is "invisible" will come up again later but consider what these statements mean about

---

[12] Matthew 22:20, Mark 12:16, Luke 20:24.

Jesus. When people saw Jesus, they saw the Father, who is otherwise unseen. Seeing Jesus—who was embodied in human flesh, and later embodied with the first of the resurrection bodies (1 Cor. 15:49)—was like seeing the Father. The Gospel of John records Jesus' statement: "He who has seen me has seen the Father; how can you say 'show us the Father'?" (Jn. 14:9). Just before that, Jesus told the apostles that seeing him and seeing the Father were one and the same (Jn. 14:7).

I wonder: what should that tell us about the Father? An "image" is only an image if it references something else that could potentially be seen. You cannot have an image of something that has no appearance. This is precisely what caused the well-known Anglican archbishop, Richard Chenevix Trench, to say that the term *eikón* "assumes a prototype, of which it not merely resembles, but from which it is drawn."[13] As if that statement is not telling enough, the renowned biblical scholar, F.F. Bruce, recorded the following: "(*eikón*) then is more than a 'shadow'; rather it is a *replication*."[14] You see, the term that was used to describe the ways in which we resemble our Creator was not supposed to subtly compare the "spiritual," interior qualities we possess. Rather, it was meant to describe the fact that we are copies of the great, uncreated Prototype. It describes the fact that we are not merely shadows of God but are something closer to being replications of Him. The early Church Father, Irenaeus, displayed his agreement with this notion in his highly-influential work, *Against Heresies*:

> "Now God shall be glorified in His handiwork, fitting it so as to be conformable to, and modelled after, His own Son. For by the hands of the Father, that is, by the Son and the Holy Spirit, man, and not [merely] a part of man, was made in the likeness of God. Now the soul and the spirit are certainly a part of the man, but certainly not the man; for the perfect man consists in the commingling and the union of the soul

---

[13] See Strong's, 1504.
[14] Ibid.

receiving the spirit of the Father, and the admixture of that fleshly nature which was moulded after the image of God."[15]

We are not God, nor are we exactly like Him. But—and this is an emphatic *but*—there is no denying that we strongly resemble our Creator. As Irenaeus alluded to, this resemblance even includes our physical existence.

What about the Hebrew term *demuth*—is there a Greek parallel for that as well? Yes, there is. This is where the previously mentioned word *homoióma* reenters the conversation. Like *demuth*, translators typically interpret *homoióma* as "likeness," but it can also be viewed as "image" or "similitude." The term is only used six times throughout the New Testament, which is less than one-fourth of the times its Hebrew equivalent is used in the Old Testament. Of those six occurrences, four are found in Paul's letter to the Romans; clearly, it had special significance there. It is first used in 1:23, when the Gentiles are shamed for having traded the worship of Yahweh for the worship of images of other human beings (emperor worship comes to mind at that time) and even animals. 5:14 displays a more figurative usage of the term, as it describes those believers who had not sinned in the "likeness" (or, in the way) that Adam had. 6:5 seems to keep with a more symbolic interpretation in that it compares the way we will take on the "likeness" of both Jesus' death and resurrection.

The final use of the term in Romans is found in 8:3. Here, we are told that Jesus was sent "in the likeness of human flesh." This sounds identical to its usage in Philippians 2:7, where it is said that Jesus was made in the "likeness" of man. Finally, the book of Revelation uses the term *homoióma* just once, where it describes the physical appearance of the locusts in John's vision (9:7). These six examples provide us with some very important information. The first thing it tells us is that the term *homoióma*—like the other terms we have looked at—can certainly work in a more figurative way. It can be used to compare the actions or characteristics

---

[15] Irenaeus, *Against Heresies*, book 5.6.1.

of two things in ways that don't necessarily have anything to do with appearances. However, it typically does not function in such a way. Instead, *homoióma*, and the other biblical words comparable to it, are most often used to describe the outer appearance of things.

The point of evaluating the previous terms that we translate as "image," "likeness," or in other ways, should be rather obvious by now. When the biblical authors made these associations, they *typically* intended us to take the terms at face-value; an image is really a tangible replica or a copy of something else, and a likeness includes a physical comparison between two things. I have just shown a plethora of places where these words are used throughout the Bible and, for the most part, they describe the physical form or appearance of the items they pertain to. With this demonstrated, there can be little doubt that many interpreters have attempted to "over-spiritualize" the idea of what it means to be made in both the image and the likeness of something else. In doing so, they have stripped away the most basic (and intended) meaning of these words. To many Christians, we only *vaguely* resemble—both in form and in function— the God that we are said to *strongly* resemble. As a result, we have lost a very important part of what it means to be made in God's image, and according to His likeness.

A Simple Kind of God

Though you probably won't hear a sermon on this particular topic next Sunday, or talk about it at the next small group meeting, there has historically been a way of understanding God known as "Divine Simplicity." On this line of reasoning, God is "simple." Now, this does not mean that God is alleged to be easy to understand or to comprehend. Far from it. Rather, Divine Simplicity is intended to mean that God is not made up of any parts. Unlike created beings, God is not comprised of attributes or faculties. Instead, God literally *is* the attributes and faculties that we would normally attribute to Him. God doesn't possess strength; He is strength.

God doesn't possess mercy; He is mercy. God doesn't possess knowledge; He is all knowledge. If you are like me, you are probably wondering what possible point these kinds of distinctions are supposed to make. What does it mean that God *is* a power or an attribute, rather than that He possesses some power or attribute? You got me. But then, that's probably why the doctrine of Divine Simplicity has been hotly contested throughout the centuries.

Divine Simplicity does not only apply to God's attributes, of course. If God really is "simple," meaning that He is not comprised of parts or qualities, then it is apparent that this overall concept must apply to God's outward existence as well. This means—as you may have guessed—that God has no tangible body or body parts, either. God has no arms, legs, head, nose, ears, mouth, hair, or anything else; He is completely and utterly immaterial. God is incorporeal—a term which *nowhere* exists in the Bible, mind you—[16] in every way, shape, and form. One of the foremost defenders of Divine Simplicity, Origen, summarized this notion for us within the first couple centuries of church history:

> "Having refuted, then, as well as we could, every notion which might suggest that we were to think of God as in any degree corporeal, we go on to say that, according to strict truth, God is incomprehensible, and incapable of being measured. For whatever be the knowledge which we are able to obtain of God, either by perception or reflection, we must of necessity believe that He is by many degrees far better than what we perceive Him to be."[17]

As Origen explained, if God is considered to exist in some "measurable" way—say, if He had appendages that could hypothetically be measured—then He would not abide by the correct standards of godliness. We must "of necessity" believe that God is unimaginably great

---

[16] See Paulsen's, *Early Christian Belief in an Embodied God: Part II*, 55.
[17] Origen, *De Principiis*, book 1.1.5.

beyond all level of description. Trust me: I know how appealing parts of this can sound. We praise God continuously for His greatness and His surpassing power, knowledge, mercy, and many other qualities. But if you read Origen's statement completely, you find that he was not simply saying that God is exceedingly great. Rather, he was saying that God is impossible to understand altogether. He said this directly; God is "incomprehensible," meaning that we cannot really begin to wrap our minds around His nature. But according to Origen, we know two things for sure about God. We know that God is incorporeal (He does not possess a body of any sort). That, in itself, is curious because we aren't supposed to be able to fully understand *anything* about God. However, we also know that God is an unembodied *mind*.

How do we know that? Well, we know that God is an unembodied mind because Origen (among others) made this clear:

> "But mind, for its movements or operations, needs no physical space, nor sensible magnitude, nor bodily shape, nor colour, nor any other of those adjuncts which are the properties of body or matter."[18]

A "mind" (i.e., God) occupies no space, magnitude, bodily shape, color, or anything that can be associated with matter. As far as we can determine, God has no relation to the world we live in, or our understanding of it. But surely, Origen had an extreme view of things. He must have been a radical of the ancient world. There isn't any way that other prominent Christian thinkers have (or do) feel the same way: that God is "simple," incomprehensible, immaterial, etc. We can rest assured that there are.

William Lane Craig—who is one of the most prominent Christian thinkers and apologists of our era—has spent considerable time writing and discussing the nature of God. While he has openly (and rightly) challenged the doctrine of Divine Simplicity—even saying that ". . . the doctrine of divine simplicity is one that has no biblical support at all and,

---

[18] Ibid. Section 6.

in my opinion, has no good philosophical arguments in its favor"—[19] his view on the incorporeality of God has been equally obvious. According to Craig, God is an ". . . uncaused, beginningless, changeless, immaterial, timeless, spaceless, and enormously powerful cause. . .."[20] Craig has also consistently referred to God as an "unembodied mind."[21] In order to have created our material universe, it is thought that God would need to be the type of being described above. Without question, this view sounds eerily similar to Origen's explanation that was previously mentioned. But ask yourself, would God need to be all those things—in particular, immaterial and unembodied—to create our universe? I have always been puzzled as to why an immaterial being is more fit to create something than a material being. Of course, the only types of beings we know of are material beings, and the only type of minds we know of are the embodied variety.

Perhaps this would be a good point to stop and take stock of what we are seeing. Consider the cost of believing in a God who is incorporeal, unembodied, and immaterial: a God without any physical "parts." It is easy to describe God in such a way, but much more difficult to assess the implications of doing so. In order to get that type of deity, you have to strip away all semblance of rationality. God is nothing like a being we can really relate to, or even imagine. In fact, God actually sounds much more like nothing at all. I mean, literally *nothing*. Besides describing the concept of "nothing" as the "absence of something," how else could we define it? I'll give it a try. How about immaterial, timeless, spaceless, unembodied, colorless, beginningless, changeless, uncaused, and not having "any other of those adjuncts which are the properties of body or matter." Does that sound familiar?

---

[19] William Lane Craig, "Divine Simplicity."
[20] William Lane Craig, "Is the Cause of the Universe an Uncaused, Personal Creator of the Universe?"
[21] See Craig's, "Is the Notion of an Unembodied Mind Defensible?" for a great example of this.

As is typically the case, the unembodied crowd was not the first to arrive at the party, nor were they even the biggest group there. I have previously shown—and will continue to show—that the Bible describes those in heaven (even God) as tangible and embodied. Church history reveals a sizeable number of people whom the self-proclaimed *eruditi* (the "educated" people) referred to as the *simpliciores* (the "simple" folk), and they also typically believed that heavenly beings had bodies.[22] Put another way, the intellectual "elite" have always felt compelled to purge the foolish people among them of their absurd beliefs. I suppose that people like Peter, John, James, and most of the biblical writers would qualify as *simpliciores* as well. I will return to this at the end of chapter two. We understand this dynamic to be true, because of the innumerable (and ubiquitous) attempts among theologians to explain away literal biblical events as metaphor. However, we also know because several of the *eruditi* specifically referenced this issue.

The early Church Father, Basil of Caesarea, defended his followers from the belief that God has form, saying: "If we have been created in the image of God, some say, God must have the same form as we . . . Do not circumscribe God with corporeal concepts, do not confine him with your mind."[23] That's right: we won't tolerate any dissenters in these parts, will we, Basil? Origen would no doubt have concurred, as would have thinkers like Augustine and Aquinas. While it is a step too far to believe that God (especially the Father) has an identical body to our own, that is not what Basil was really rejecting; he was rejecting that any "corporeal concepts" can be applied to God at all. Apparently, many of the subjects under Basil's tutelage had naïvely come to believe in nonsense like the plain reading—that is, how the biblical authors clearly intended it to be understood—of Scripture.

Similar lectures about the foolishness of believing in an embodied deity are scattered throughout the first several centuries of church history.

---

[22] Griffin and Paulsen, "Simpliciores, Eruditi, and the Noetic Form of God."
[23] Griffin and Paulsen, "Augustine and the Corporeality of God," 102.

One particularly telling example is when a man named Theophilus sent a letter to the churches in Egypt around 399 A.D., scolding the believers there for accepting that God had form or shape. The Christian monk, John Cassian, chronicled the response of those who were being criticized. It was recorded that the letter

> ". . . was received very bitterly by almost every sort of monk throughout all Egypt . . . indeed, the majority of the older men among the brethren asserted that in fact the bishop was to be condemned as someone corrupted by the most serious heresy, someone opposing the ideas of holy Scripture, someone who denied that almighty God was of human shape and this despite the clear scriptural evidence that Adam was created in His image."[24]

To those Theophilus addressed in Egypt, believing that God had tangible form of some type was a foregone conclusion. They believed it was Theophilus who was not following the teachings of Scripture, not them. They were probably right.

It was not just Christian groups during the first several hundred years after the death of Christ who believed God has tangible form, either. If we consider the Jewish teachings on the matter during that time, we see that they largely held to the Old Testament perspective on the matter. Scholar of Jewish studies, Alon Goshen Gottstein, has succinctly summarized this:

> "In all of rabbinic literature [covering both the tannaitic (70-200 A.D.) and amoraic (220-500 A.D.) periods] there is not a single statement that categorically denies that God has body or form. In my understanding, the question of whether the rabbis believed in a God who has form is one that needs little discussion . . . Instead of asking, 'Does God have a

---

[24] See Luibhéid's, *John Cassian: Conferences,* 125-126, for more on this.

body?' we should inquire, 'What kind of body does God have?' "[25]

Indeed: what *kind* of body does God have? I will begin to address this in the next section, and throughout many parts of the book afterwards. This proves to be an interesting point though. For a great many believers in history, the question was never about whether God exists in some type of physical form or embodiment. To them, this was an obvious belief when we consider the biblical information available to us. Instead, they had moved to an attempt to better understand the connection that exists between God and His physical form.

If the biblical authors, the ancient Jewish people, most of the rabbinic teachings of the day, and a significant number of the earliest Christians all believed in the corporeal nature of God, what happened? What exactly caused so many believers thereafter—particularly from among the *eruditi*—to conclude that God is unembodied and incorporeal? After spending considerable time investigating the reasons why it is believed that we possess a soul that can consciously live apart from the body—which I will specifically discuss in the first part of chapter four—I was not surprised that many others view God as immaterial, incorporeal, unembodied, and whatever additional terms one might opt to add. It was not shocking because the same general principles and underlying assumptions are present within both beliefs. In essence, Platonic (and Neoplatonic) beliefs are the backbone of this view. This notion comes to us from Greek philosophy, not biblical theology. In an article printed in the *Harvard Review*, theologians Carl Griffin and David Paulsen summarized this reality quite clearly:

> "Platonists believed, unlike the Stoics, that there were intellectual principles which existed independently from matter. In the hierarchy of being these 'ideas' were superior to their material

---

[25] Alon Gottstein, "The Body as Image of God in Rabbinic Literature," 172.

instances, and above them all was the One, or God, who was necessarily incorporeal and, as their source, beyond intellect and matter. The fundaments of Platonic physics and metaphysics came to be regarded by most educated people in Late Antiquity as self-evident, which is why so many Christian and pagan philosophers alike found utterly unintelligible the suggestion that God was corporeal or material."[26]

This assessment is exactly right. I would add that this type of reasoning is also why many Christians believe that our souls will one day depart and live independent from our bodies.

Paulsen further clarifies the reasons why many of the spiritual cognoscenti came to steadfastly reject God's corporeality:

"Christians for at least the first three centuries of the current era commonly (and perhaps generally) believed God to be corporeal. The belief was abandoned (and then only gradually) as Neoplatonism became more and more entrenched as the dominant worldview of Christian thinkers."[27]

As Neoplatonism—with its emphasis on the immaterial over the material—began to become a common fixture within the church, so too did the belief that God is an unembodied being.

In a discussion concerning man's stewardship of Creation, the well-known theologian, Francis Schaeffer, once expressed the consequences of this worldview very clearly:

"Any Christianity that rests upon a dichotomy—some sort of platonic concept—simply does not have an answer to nature, and we must say with tears that much orthodoxy, much evangelical Christianity, is rooted in a platonic concept wherein the only interest is in the 'upper story,' in the heavenly things—only in 'saving the soul' and getting it to heaven. In this platonic

---

[26] Ibid. 103
[27] Paulsen, "Early Christian Belief in a Corporeal Deity."

concept, even though orthodox and evangelical terminology is used, there is little or no interest in proper pleasures of the body or proper uses of the intellect."[28]

As Schaeffer noted, the undeniable influence of Platonic thought within the church is not only real but has largely been a detriment to Christian teaching. This applies to our attempt at "escapism"—whereby we feel as though we can leave the world to ruin because we (our souls) will someday escape it—and it most definitely applies to our conceptions of both God and the angels as being unembodied beings. We must be absolutely clear here: the catalyst for this shift was *not* the words of Christ, the apostles, or the prophets, but the teachings of prominent Greek philosophers and their adherents. As is too often the case, the authors of the biblical texts have not influenced the beliefs of the church as strongly as their secular or non-believing contemporaries have. The vast majority of Bible-believers are completely in the dark as to how profound an impact secular philosophy has had on their personal beliefs, and the beliefs of the church at large. I continue to be astonished by how deep these roots descend.

Lower than the Angels

One of the very most intriguing aspects of reality is that we are not alone in it. While it may be true—so far as we can tell—that we are alone in the universe, we certainly are not the only entities who exist *anywhere*. The Bible is abundantly clear that God created other beings at some point in the history of His workings, and we call these beings "angels." Though, like us, the angels came to exist a finite time ago—they are not eternal and uncaused, as we believe God to be—they clearly hold a more privileged position than we do. They live with God in the heavenly realm, and we do not. They share a closeness to God that we are not yet able to enjoy, but

---

[28] Francis Schaeffer, *Pollution and the Death of Man*, 40.

someday will. But what is involved in this "closeness" they share with the Almighty? Could this, in some way, shape, or form, have something to do with their physical makeup and their spatial location? More than that, do we share any similarities with them?

In the previous sections, I made it clear why I believe that God has a body. After the Incarnation and the Resurrection, that belief proves to be undeniably true; since the Son of God exists in bodily form, physical existence is a reality within the Trinity. But I propose that God was connected to substantive existence—meaning that God somehow, and in some way, had tangible qualities—before that. Precisely what type of body this would be is the topic of the next section, and I will tell you in advance that I do not know the answer to that question to a certainty. On a less provocative note, I also believe that we are embodied beings. At least there won't be any resistance on that particular point! But what of those other beings? What about the angels: are they also embodied? On the surface, this question seems to be as easy to answer as the question about whether God is embodied. *No* . . . of course the angels don't have bodies. Like God, they are incorporeal. That is no doubt the standard teaching on the matter, though I doubt most of us have ever been taught *why* this is believed to be the case. I am afraid that viewing the angels as immaterial beings—meaning they have no physicality or spatial extension—is neither a biblical nor logical proposition.

For starters, just consider the first time an angel ever appears in Scripture without a body. Recall that moment of surprise when a human being is recorded to have been visited by an unembodied being from heaven. If you are having trouble placing this passage of Scripture, you are in good company. You cannot place it, because it doesn't exist. Like God's appearances in the Bible, there is not a single recorded verse that would really indicate that angels are immaterial entities. I mean, how could an immaterial being "show up" to anyone? What is there to see, hear, or touch? This is where defenders of this view would chime in, saying something like this: "that's because the angels *temporarily manifest* themselves to us, but they are otherwise unembodied!" That would make good sense, if it weren't for that fact that there is no credible reason to believe it. There is no indication within the Bible that these physical appearances are the exceptions to the rule, and that angels (or God) return to a non-physical state after visiting us. Beyond inserting several thousand years of philosophical thought into the biblical texts, we have no real basis to believe it. However, we do have more than ample reason to believe the contrary.

I already mentioned the incredible appearance of the angels to Elisha and his servant in 2 Kings 6:16-17, which not only reveals to us that heaven is a realm of existence—albeit, one that is typically invisible to our sight—but also that the angels are tangible entities. Upon close examination, every other angelic visitation described within the Bible is similar in type. Angels, appearing in bodily form, came to Abraham at Mamre (Gen. 18:1-2). Angels later appeared to Abraham's nephew, Lot, prior to the Sodom and Gomorrah disaster (Gen. 19:1-22). Jacob and Ezekiel both had visions of angels—which were indicative of what they actually look like—at crucial times in their lives (Gen. 28:12, Ez. 1:1-28). King David encountered a destroying angel that even possessed some type of sword (1 Chr. 21). This is just to name a few of the possible examples we could look at within the Old Testament.

If we look to the New Testament, we also hear only of embodied beings. Angels appeared to the women who had come to anoint Jesus' body at the empty tomb, after the Resurrection (Mk. 16:1-8). Two angels appeared again to those who witnessed the Ascension (Acts 1:10-11). The angel Gabriel appeared to Zechariah in order to tell him that he and Elizabeth would bear a son named John (Lk. 1:5-20). Later on, Gabriel appeared to Mary as well, telling her that she would be giving birth to the Messiah himself (Lk. 1:26-38). I could continue to list the places where angels physically appeared throughout biblical history, but there is no need to beat a dead horse. The fact is that the Bible always describes the angels as having bodies. In order to make the case that they are actually immaterial beings who occasionally appear physically, one needs to reject all the evidence in hand. We are told that they appear as embodied beings. We are not told that they are otherwise immaterial.

One of the most unusual connections that exists between human beings and angels involves how the latter are described within the Bible. A moment ago, I mentioned that two angels visited those who had seen Jesus disappear into the heavens for the last time (Acts 1:10-11). However, there is something peculiar that was not mentioned. Just after Jesus ascended, the following event occurred:

> "And as they were gazing intently into the sky while He was going, behold, two men in white clothing stood beside them. They also said, 'Men of Galilee, why do you stand looking into the sky? This Jesus, who has been taken up from you into heaven, will come in just the same way as you have watched Him go into heaven.'"

Did you notice what the text literally says: that two *men* stood beside them? Why does it say "men" if we are supposed to be dealing with angels? In order to answer that question, we will need to look at some other events in Scripture.

Let's journey backwards in the Bible to the situation concerning Lot and the destruction of Sodom and Gomorrah. This strange ordeal will come up again in chapter three, when I discuss the matter of the Nephilim (giants) and what they tell us about our relationship to the angels. At present, there is something else we need to glean from this event. Genesis introduces Lot's two prophetic visitors very clearly as heavenly messengers: "Now the two angels came to Sodom in the evening as Lot was sitting in the gate of Sodom" (19:1). Later on, they are again referred to as angels (19:15). We can also be sure these were not mere mortals because of Lot's reaction to their arrival. "When Lot saw them, he rose to meet them and bowed down with his face to the ground. And he said, 'Now behold, my lords, please turn aside into your servant's house' . . ." (19:1-2). If there should be any remaining doubts that these were indeed beings of a higher power, the text records that they miraculously blinded the men from Sodom, after they had tried to break into the house (19:11). I don't know of any human beings who could have accomplished this.

However, this is not the end of the matter. The same account describes Lot's two friends just a bit differently: as "men." In fact, this occurs in three different ways: 1) The group from Sodom called them "men" (19:5); 2) Lot called them "men" (19:8); and 3) The narrator/author of Genesis called them "men" (19:10, 12). The reasons why the group from Sodom was so interested in the angels is another matter, which will also later be addressed. At the moment, that is beside the point. If you are thinking that the men being referenced in those verses are not the same as the two entities who are elsewhere described as angels, think again. If you read the account carefully, it is obvious that the two "men" who pulled Lot back into the house (19:10) were the same figures who blinded those who were outside of the house (19:11). Moreover, the two "men" that asked Lot who else was living with him (19:12) were the same individuals that claimed they would later destroy the city (19:13). Clearly, that was a supernatural event.

This cannot be right, can it? Is there some type of mistake in the wording, or perhaps an issue with our translation of the Hebrew text? Incredibly, there is not. The word that is translated as "angels" is from the same term (*malak*) that is used throughout the Old Testament to describe them. Likewise, the term (*ish*) used to simultaneously describe them as "men" means exactly that throughout the OT. In no uncertain terms, Lot's foreign company are described as both men and angels in this story. But there is even more going on here. Prior to Lot's encounter with the two visitors, Abraham also met with them (18:1-15). However, there is very strange twist involved in Abraham's experience: the Lord (Yahweh) also appeared to him. As in Lot's story, the heavenly visitors even enjoyed a substantial meal together (18:5-8).

What is by far the most incredible aspect of this account is that the Lord was also described as—you guessed it—a *man* (18:2). Nearly everyone who has commented on or attempted to explain this phenomenon says the same thing: both God and the angels simply assumed something like a human form, but do not typically possess one. Some even suggest that this appearance of Yahweh was the Son of God, who is often believed to be the "angel of the Lord" figure that appears throughout the OT.[29] I have more to say about this in the next chapter. However, it needs to be stated now that viewing the Lord's appearance to Abraham as a manifestation of the Son of God falls flat for two primary reasons. The first is that 18:1 mentions nothing about an angel (*malak*) but mentions only Yahweh (*Yhvh*), which is God's proper name in the OT. The second is that such a distinction is irrelevant, because the primary motive for making this claim is to keep the Father unembodied. To some, there is a perceived logical advantage to granting the Son—who is also fully divine—embodiment while refusing it to the Father. For the life of me, I don't know what that is supposed to achieve.

Moving on, the main point is that both God and the two angels appeared to Abraham and Lot in bodily form and were all called "men" at certain times. Now, some readers may be thinking: "Well, even if that is the case, these examples must be anomalies. Surely, they are just the products of strange events or circumstances." When we consider the harassment on display by the men of Sodom, the city's fiery destruction, and Abraham's meeting with the Lord and His two companions, these are certainly difficult events to comprehend. The oddity of these situations might be able to account for the comparison between men and angels, if it weren't for the fact that it is a discernible theme throughout the Bible.

We already saw this with the "men in white clothing" who appeared at the Ascension (Acts 1:10-11). There can be little doubt that these were angelic beings, because they appeared from nowhere and wore white clothing. Appearing in white clothing is an allusion almost exclusively

---

[29] See *Mathew Henry's Commentary* on 18:2, for example: "These were three heavenly beings in human bodies. Some think they were all created angels; others, that one of them was the Son of God, the Angel of the covenant."

pertaining to heavenly beings, whether that be Jesus, angels, or even those who will be purified and saved.[30] Speaking of white clothing, the three women who came to anoint Jesus' body the morning after the Crucifixion also encountered a person wearing such attire:

> "Entering the tomb, they saw a young man sitting at the right, wearing a white robe; and they were amazed. And he said to them, 'Do not be amazed; you are looking for Jesus the Nazarene, who has been crucified. He has risen; He is not here; behold, here is the place where they laid Him' " (Mk. 16:5-6).

Curiously, this time we are dealing with a *neaniskon*: a "young man." Could this mean that certain angels start out younger than others, and that some type of aging exists even among the heavenly beings? Or, could it be that his particular appearance just seemed a bit more youthful by human standards? It is very difficult to say what the significance of him being a "young man" is within this passage. Whatever the case, it is clear to see that he too was not of this world. We know this because of his white robe, his supernatural understanding of all that had transpired, and because of the women's reactions to him. The word used here for "amazed" (*exethambēthēsan*) is very emphatic. It is used—in one form or another—only in Mark's gospel, and only four times within that.[31] It could also mean "awe-struck" or "greatly amazed," but carries with it the idea of being shocked to the point of fright.[32] Accordingly, we read how the women responded to the surprise of Jesus being absent from the tomb and their encounter with the being in white: "They went out and fled from the tomb, for trembling and astonishment had gripped them; and they said nothing to anyone, for they were afraid" (16:8). This was no mere mortal whom they had encountered.

---

[30] For some excellent examples of the types of beings who are dressed in white, see the following verses: Mt. 17:2, 28:3; Jn. 20:12; Rev. 1:14, 3:4, 6:11, and 7:9.
[31] See 9:15, 14:33, 16:5, and 16:6.
[32] Strong's Concordance, 1568: "ekthambeó."

I would be remiss if I did not include Jacob's legendary battle with a strange opponent. Genesis 32:24-32 describes the entire ordeal clearly. There, Jacob—who had been left alone for the evening—encountered what Genesis calls a "man" (*enosh*), with whom he proceeded to physically quarrel with all night until daybreak (32:24). Famously, Jacob refused to let the man go until he had received a blessing, even though he had been badly wounded. As a result, the visitor blessed Jacob and changed his name to "Israel" (32:28). Obviously, this name would have everlasting significance. Two things really stand out after the altercation, however. The first is the man's rationale behind changing Jacob's name: "Your name shall no longer be Jacob, but Israel; for you have striven with God and with men and have prevailed" (32:28). Second, Jacob then institutes a name of his own, this time to the location where all this had transpired: "So Jacob named the place Peniel, for *he said*, 'I have seen God face to face, yet my life has been preserved' " (32:30). Peniel (or Penuel, probably) means something close to "face of God." Another curious facet of the story is that Jacob in turn asked the man what his name was, to which the man responded in an almost rhetorical way: "Why is it that you ask my name?" (32:29). This seems to be the man's way of saying, "you know full-well who *I am*. I am who I am!" This fits with the idea that Jacob's wrestling partner may have been God Himself, and some translations even label the passage with titles like "Jacob Wrestles with God."[33]

Not surprisingly, there has always been debate about who Jacob actually faced off against. Despite what was previously said, the Bible itself does not offer full clarity on the matter. If we look at the book attributed to the prophet Hosea, there is an allusion to Jacob's battle with the man. There, however, the being is not referred to as a man, but as an angel (*malak*): "Yes, he wrestled with the angel and prevailed . . ." (Hos. 12:4). While it is difficult to imagine, the Bible refers to Jacob's adversary (and

---

[33] See the ESV, NLT, and NIV, for some examples. The NASB, perhaps wisely, simply titles this section, "Jacob Wrestles." With the ambiguity surrounding the passage, this feels vague but appropriate.

benefactor) as a man, an angel, and even as God. Whether directly stated or just implied, all three descriptions are present. In the end, we simply don't know exactly what to make of this character. However—and this is the most important part—we can be sure about what this being *was not*; this was not just a normal man. Whoever it was, the figure had a heavenly origin. We also know that we have, in this passage, another place where there is a strong biblical connection between human beings and celestial beings.

All this information meshes with what we can learn from Jesus' resurrection and his appearances thereafter. Since this will be discussed several times in the book, and in detail towards the end of this chapter, I will not elaborate here and now. It will become apparent that, while Jesus had unquestionably been changed after the Resurrection, he still looked rather human. He did not appear exactly as the mortal man he had previously been, but he also did not look like some entirely different type of creature. Hopefully, it will also become apparent that Jesus now possesses a body of the same fashion that the angels have, and we will someday have.

Though it may be difficult to wrap our minds around—particularly because this is not how things are normally taught—the close connection between human beings and angels is extremely difficult to ignore. The biblical authors most definitely believed there to be profound similarities between the human form and the angelic form. Later in the book, I will discuss other ways that these similarities overlap, and they range from the unusual to the downright bizarre. For now, perhaps all this can help us to make sense of the enigmatic statement in Hebrews 13:2: "Do not neglect to show hospitality to strangers, for by this some have entertained angels without knowing it." Could it be that angels are sometimes among us, and that they are able to blend in because they are very much like us? Another passage from Hebrews that now reads a lot differently is 2:5-9. Within that section, the following is recorded:

"What is mankind that you are mindful of them, a son of man that you care for him? You made them a little lower than the angels; you crowned them with glory and honor and put everything under their feet" (2:6-8, NIV).

This is virtually a direct quote from Psalm 8:5. The point here in Hebrews is that everything in the world was created for human beings to rule, though our disjointed world does not bear that out at present. It goes on to suggest that Jesus remedied that situation on our behalf, and that even he was "made lower than the angels for a little while" (2:9). The point is that our appearance is not an unrecognizable step down from the angelic form. Not only were we made in God's image, but the angels were as well.

At the close of this section, we have reached a critical juncture. Since it is undeniable—from a biblical perspective, at least—that angels and humans resemble one another, what are we to make of this? Really, there are two possibilities for how we might view this matter. The first is to believe that the angels are discussed as being human-like, even to the point of being called "men" in many places, because they *intermittently* appear in our likeness. They do not authentically have bodies and resemble human beings; they only occasionally appear like this as a way of reaching out and making sense to us. As I will unpack throughout the book, this tends to be the default position within most parts of the church. At the least, it is the position held by a large number of Christian apologists and philosophers. The alternative is to believe that angels resemble human beings in many respects *because they actually do*. That is, there is no trick at play; angels and humans both share in God's image, and there is a physical component to this reality. If true, this would mean that the biblical authors described the angels just as they truly are. They neither described things incorrectly nor intended that we apply a philosophical layer over top of their words in order to ascertain the truth. Hopefully, you will be able to determine which view makes the most sense as we continue. One thing is for sure though: we are presently a little lower than the angels. Of course, one day that could all change. We can never forget Paul's mysterious words in 1 Corinthians 6:3: "Do you not know that we will judge angels?"

No*body* Knows

While it should be obvious at this point that I believe both God and the angels to be embodied beings (in some way), I want to be very clear that I do not believe that God is a flesh and bone being *exactly* like us. As is usually the case, we need to be very clear (and very careful) about what we are saying on this topic. We are talking about the very nature of our Creator, after all. There is no question that the Bible—particularly the Old Testament—often describes God anthropomorphically. More accurately, we could say that the Bible describes humanity "theomorphically." That is, we are formed in the image of God and are like Him, not the other way around. Getting back to the anthropomorphic issue, God is recurrently portrayed as having human-like traits, characteristics, and even body parts. I will discuss some of these momentarily, as I do believe they tell us at least something about the actual nature of God. But if we remember the Greek and Hebrew words that were evaluated earlier in the chapter, the biblical authors intended us to think of appearances as a connection we share with God. However, the words they used were not meant to express things that are—in all ways—*identical* in nature or appearance. An image shares great similarity with the item it is crafted to resemble, but it is not precisely the same. The Mona Lisa mirrors the person (Lisa Gherardini) that Leonardo da Vinci modeled it after, but the painting is not actually the woman herself, nor does the painting share her identical form or appearance; it is comprised of oil and poplar wood, and was certainly not created exactly to scale. We would be wrong to jettison all notions about the tangible nature of God, but we would be equally incorrect in believing that God's form or appearance is just like our own.

This is an incredibly important point to understand, since there seems to be a theological disdain for anthropomorphic suggestions. I could not begin to tell you how many times I have heard someone say, "we can't anthropomorphize God." How dare we talk about God in human terms! I previously demonstrated that there has been a genuine fear among theologians and philosophers to compare God to anything or to offer any firm descriptions about Him. Origen served as a prominent example from antiquity and William Lane Craig as a more modern voice, among others.

The Greek philosophy that has so informed the post-apostolic church again enters the picture. I recall Saint Augustine's words on the nature of God:

> "I thought not of Thee, O God, under the figure of a human body; since I began to hear aught of wisdom, I always avoided this; and rejoiced to have found the same in the faith of our spiritual mother, Thy Catholic Church. But what else to conceive of Thee I knew not. And I, a man, and such a man, sought to conceive of Thee the sovereign, only, true God; and I did in my inmost soul believe that Thou wert incorruptible, and uninjurable, and unchangeable; because though not knowing whence or how, yet I saw plainly, and was sure, that that which may be corrupted must be inferior to that which cannot; what could not be injured I preferred unhesitatingly to what could receive injury; the unchangeable to things subject to change."[34]

I realize that a lot of that paragraph is difficult to understand. In truth, it is for most of us (if we are being honest). However, two things come to the surface in those statements. The "aught of wisdom" that caused Augustine to reject the notion of an embodied God was probably the prevailing Greek philosophical perspectives on the matter. Augustine believed that God must be "incorruptible," "uninjurable," and *unchangeable*. As an extension of that reality, Augustine revealed something that was absolutely fundamental

---

[34] Augustine, "Confessions," chapter 7.

in his thinking: ". . . that which may be corrupted must be inferior to that which cannot." And what does that mean? Well, it basically means that material things—since they are all thought to change and decay—must be inferior to immaterial things. For Augustine, the physical world seemed to point naturally to an immaterial world (with immaterial beings) that is ultimately superior to our (or any conceivable) material world. Indeed, many of the Greek philosophers from antiquity would be very proud of Mr. Augustine.

I mention this influence again here because it has much to do with the fear of anthropomorphizing God: of describing Him as being somehow similar to us. As we are all aware, humans are material beings who inhabit a material world. Based on the previous perspectives we have seen, it would be absurd to view God in any way that may be construed as human-like, because that would bring matter into the mix. Compared to the Greek philosophical beliefs about ideal forms and perfection, a tangible and embodied deity could never obtain this type of status. Matter—of any type, apparently even the heavenly variety—is bound to decay, deteriorate and change. I cannot be more emphatic: this way of thinking is the underlying reason why there is anxiety in talking about an embodied God, or in describing God as possessing any physical similarities with us. But here is the major problem: it was not we who anthropomorphized God, but God who anthropomorphized Himself.

Think about it for a moment: did the biblical authors errantly describe God anthropomorphically? Or, did they secretly intend that we take all such descriptions figuratively? Recall God's words to Moses at Mt. Sinai: "You cannot see My face, for no man can see Me and live!" (Ex. 33:20). This reminds me a great deal of John's statements early in his gospel: "No one has seen God at any time; the only begotten Son who is in the bosom of the Father, he has explained Him (1:18)" and also, "Not that anyone has seen the Father, except the One who is from God; He has seen the Father" (Jn. 6:46). Notice that all of these verses suggest that God the Father *could potentially* be seen (and has been seen by the Son).

Naturally, these are not meant to be taken literally. That is what we're told, anyway. Of course, I would love for someone to explain the "figurative" meaning of these verses. What purpose would God possibly have had in referring to a body that He doesn't literally possess? I don't have slightest idea. "Hey, Moses, no one can look upon my face and live to tell about it! I'm only kidding; there's nothing to see here. I was just showing my allegorical side." I suppose John was waxing poetic, too. The Son had not *really* seen the Father; the word "seen" was merely being used to suggest that the Son "deeply understands" Him, or some such nonsense.

To take this one step further, let's quickly take a closer look at Exodus 33. I invite you to read that chapter for yourself (it is very short). You will find that there is absolutely nothing about the text that appears to be metaphorical or figurative. The events recorded in Exodus 33 read as historical narrative through and through. Right before the events of this section was the infamous golden calf incident, where the Israelites made a false idol to worship. As a result, God struck the people with a plague (32:35), but later began to instruct the people about how to make it to the land of Canaan (the "Promised Land"). In a special meeting place—called the "Tent of Meeting"—it is said that "the Lord used to speak to Moses face to face, as a man speaks to his friend" (33:11).

Later in the narrative, Moses asks to see God's "glory"—which I take to mean that he wanted to see God in all His splendor and fullness, being that Moses was already interacting with God so closely—and God provides Moses with a series of instructions about how the whole event would need to transpire. God would pass by Moses (33:19), but Moses would have to stand on a nearby rock (33:21). When God went by, He would place Moses in a cleft of the rock and cover him with His hand (33:22-23). As God clarified on two separate occasions, all this was necessary so that Moses would not be able to see His *face* (33:20, 23). Immediately after these amazing events, Exodus 34 tells of the creation of the new stone tablets that God would inscribe the Ten Commandments on. There, it was also noted that the Lord "passed by" Moses (34:6).

Curiously, when Moses had returned from the mountain, his face visibly shone (34:29). The word there (*qaran*) specifically means to "send out rays," and it was used almost exclusively in Exodus 34 to describe Moses' face.[35] God repeatedly showed Himself to Moses, and Moses came away with physical validation of this fact. What was figurative about any of this? Would Moses really have understood his encounters with God as metaphor: as not literally occurring? You be the judge.

While those instances are particularly problematic to the belief that God the Father is incorporeal, there are other passages to consider. God appears to Abraham on numerous occasions in the book of Genesis.[36] Jacob of course encountered God in a primitive wrestling match of sorts (Gen. 32:24-32), where he said that he had—you guessed it—seen God *face to face* (v. 30). When Moses and the Israelites affirmed their covenant with God, a most remarkable account was recorded:

> "Then Moses went up with Aaron, Nadab and Abihu, and seventy of the elders of Israel, and they saw the God of Israel; and under His feet there appeared to be a pavement of sapphire, as clear as the sky itself. Yet He did not stretch out His hand against the nobles of the sons of Israel; and they saw God, and they ate and drank."[37]

The passage twice reports that the people "saw God." Another figurative encounter, I suppose. Speaking of events that are typically seen as metaphorical, there is the time when God walked in the Garden with Adam and Eve (Gen. 3:8). Funny, many of the same interpreters who dismiss God's appearance to Adam and Eve as symbolic, anthropomorphic language, do not hesitate to take the preceding or proceeding verses quite literally (when Adam and Eve ate from the forbidden tree, when God pronounced their punishment accordingly, etc.).

---

[35] Strong's Concordance, 7160: "qaran."
[36] See 12:1-3, 12:7, 17:1, and 18:1 for some examples.
[37] Exodus 24:9-11.

Those who are honest enough to admit that these verses are not a natural fit to interpret figuratively still find interesting ways around them. Perhaps the most prominent example of this is the suggestion that every appearance of God in the Old Testament was made, in reality, by the Son and not the Father. Every time God appeared—or, namely, the "angel of the Lord" appeared—in bodily form was supposedly the Son manifesting. In other words, the pre-incarnate Word of God made himself physically known before he was born as the man Jesus. Theologian Walter Kaiser summarized Jesus' connection to the "angel of the Lord" and many of the associated appearances as follows:

> This 'Angel of the LORD' was a title that stood for his [the Son's] office, but it did not describe his nature. The Hebrew word for 'angel' (mal'ak) had the basic idea of one who was 'sent,' a 'messenger.' Of the 214 usages of the Hebrew term used for 'angel,' about one-third of them refer to what is labeled by theologians as a 'Christophany,' a temporary appearance of Christ in the Old Testament."[38]

While Kaiser did not take it so far here, many theologians have essentially asserted that every physical theophany (there are non-physical, audible contacts by God also) is actually a Christophany. God the Father never physically appears, but the Son does. This explanation is apparently supposed to make sense of John's statement that God has not been seen by any mortal being (Jn. 6:46); God the Father has never been seen, but God the Son has.

As I mentioned in the previous section, the "angel of the Lord" appears all throughout the Old Testament. He appeared to Hagar (Gen. 16:9-13), Gideon (Jdg. 6:11-24), and Samson's parents (Jdg. 13:2-23), just to name a few. While there is undoubtedly a connection between the "angel of the Lord" and God Himself, there is certainly a great deal of debate as to whether or not he is the Son of God. But in all honesty, I'm

---

[38] Walter Kaiser, "Jesus in the Old Testament" (emphasis mine).

not sure what this is supposed to achieve in the first place. Even if we grant the highly-contested points that the "angel of the Lord" *is* the Son of God, and that only the Son physically appeared in the Old Testament, it still would not yield the desired results. So, God the Father is perpetually an immaterial being, but God the Son is not. Here I thought that the Father, Son, and Spirit were supposed to be "one."

If the Son was a corporeal being, who had a physical appearance even prior to the Incarnation (when the Son became human in the man Jesus), what does that say about God as a whole? It seems that we would have to radically separate the Son from both the Father and the Spirit. That the Son supposedly has some type of physical body (and always has), while the other two members of the Trinity do not, seems to be quite a significant difference in nature. At the least, it smells like a rather disingenuous statement to say that "God"—a term we primarily use to connote all three members of the Godhead—is an immaterial, unembodied being. Further, why is it so crucial that we view the Father as being unembodied, when it is no problem to attach a body to the Son? After every visible manifestation, I suppose the Son also went back to being immaterial. Sure, why not throw that in there? As I will later show in the section entitled, *The Rise of Immaterialism*, there are people who have already made this case! In my view of things, we would be wise to drop the mental gymnastics and accept what the biblical authors revealed to us; God the Father is not incorporeal.

Hold on; wait a minute. How can we believe that God the Father possesses a physical form (as in His statement and appearances to Moses), while also admitting that "no one has seen the Father" except the Son? Well, we can affirm both beliefs because they are actually connected to one another. God's warning to Moses was that no one could see His face and live. John's statement was that no one—which we can only take to mean "no normal human being"—had ever seen God (the Father, in this context) before. If you think about it, there is no discrepancy here whatsoever. While God appeared to people "face to face" in the OT, it is

40

specifically noted that He took pains to cover or obstruct His appearance; people were really seeing God, but not fully and clearly. Moses' radiant face shows us the incredible power involved in coming near His presence at all. No human had ever seen the Father (in His fullness) because, as He told Moses, that is not something a mere mortal can handle. However, divine persons can look at other divine persons; the Father, the Son, and presumably the Spirit, can see one another. We can only assume that the angels can do so as well. It is not that it is impossible to see the Father because He is some immaterial being. Rather, it is impossible for *one of us* to do so at present. Jesus, being fully man *and* fully divine, was able to see the Father. Moses saw the Father to only a partial extent; God saw to that. Jesus has seen the Father completely, in all His glory.

To summarize the contents of this section, it seems fair to say that it was actually God who described Himself anthropomorphically. As any Bible-believing Christian can affirm, these descriptions were recorded by the biblical authors, who were inspired by God to write. The biblical characters didn't simply make all this up out of thin air. Of course, God did more than just describe Himself in human-like ways. Far more, actually. It was the Son of God who literally became a human being at a specific point in our history. And Jesus wasn't merely "sort of" like a human being. He didn't only vaguely resemble us. *Jesus was one of us, completely.* He ate, talked, laughed, loved, bled, cried, suffered, and even died, as one of us. I guess God isn't nearly as concerned with being found in human form as we are with finding Him that way.

I find it fascinating that a lot of thinkers are completely comfortable with talking about the many ways we are like God, so long as we pass our beliefs through the lens of strict immaterialism. That is, we had better not try to say that God physically exists. God and matter apparently do not mix. However, we have to try to be honest about what we are seeing. We were told early and often about these matters; "Let us make man in our image." Since about the second or third century A.D., many Christian scholars, teachers, pastors, and theologians have been trying their best to figure a way out of this reality. To many, our physical existence has no part to play in what it means to exist in God's image. Yet, God declared—and even showed us in the man Jesus, through both the Incarnation and the Resurrection—time and time again that we are very much like Him. Alternatively, we have tried time and time again to tell Him (and each other) that we are not.

Different Forms?

With all that was said in the previous section, we need to be extremely clear about what type of bodies we are talking about here. While it is a biblical certainty (I think) that the heavenly beings have bodies, it is equally obvious that these bodies are *not* identical in type to our own. Even the anthropomorphic language within the Bible, while certainly directing us towards understanding God in a physical sense, cannot be taken so far as to reduce God to being human. We are made in God's image, but we were not made to be *identical* to God. So, we are left to consider what type of bodies we were made to reflect. Fortunately, the Bible also gives us a wonderful look at the heavenly body type. We can read about the Resurrection, and about the body Jesus possessed thereafter. This will be discussed extensively in chapter four, so I will not explore this matter here and now.

Instead, we must briefly examine a strange phenomenon that the Bible at least leaves the door open to: shape-shifting. There is some reason to believe that, even though they possess bodies, the heavenly beings have the type of bodies that can appear in different forms; they are not bound to appearing in only one way. This concept is not a concrete reality within Scripture, and I would not suggest that it is. However, it is important to note this possibility because it has bearing on how we view both the embodiment and the abilities of the heavenly beings. It seems that their mode of existence is more flexible than our own, with fewer limitations.

Let's look at a few examples of where this line of thinking shows up in the Bible.

The first example worth mentioning comes to us from the final chapter of the Gospel of Mark. There, the book records that Jesus appeared to the apostles after the Resurrection. While that is not surprising—since he did so numerous times, according to the other accounts—the way in which he made himself present is a bit more startling. After his closest followers doubted that he had appeared to Mary Magdalene (16:9-11), Jesus decided to up the ante, so to speak. Mark 16:12 records the following: "After that, He appeared in a different form to two of them while they were walking along on their way to the country." This probably parallels the Road to Emmaus account in Luke 24:13-35, since Jesus appeared to two disciples there also. While they had difficulty recognizing him, they ran off to tell the others after they finally realized it was the risen Jesus. As Mark 16:13 goes on to describe, Jesus' attempt there did not result in a joyous response from the apostles; "They went away and reported it to the others, but they did not believe them either." This was par for the course, really. The gospels are emphatic about the lack of faith the apostles displayed immediately following the Crucifixion. It took many attempts for Jesus to convince them he had conquered death.

For now, the key point is that Jesus "appeared in a different form." There are really two likely explanations for this oddity. The first is the most conventional: the "different form" was just an allusion to the fact that he had come back to life with what Paul called the "spiritual body" (1 Cor. 15:44). This is synonymous with the "resurrection body." However, since Jesus had previously appeared to Mary Magdalene after the Resurrection, this interpretation is a bit less likely. Still, he had not appeared to *those* particular disciples with his new body, so we cannot discount it. The alternative is that Jesus appeared in a form different from the one he rose from the grave with. In essence, Jesus either looked different than he did prior to the Resurrection—which we know to be true from other texts—or he even looked different than he had the previous time *after* the Resurrection. Put another way, he either arrived with a second appearance or with a third appearance. There was Jesus before the Crucifixion, Jesus after the Resurrection, then perhaps Jesus in another post-Resurrection form. The term "different form" (*hetera morphē*) would normally provide us with a clue, since the term *heteros* means "another" of a *different* or *distinct* kind. In this case, however, both interpretations would have Jesus showing up in a noticeably altered form than the previous appearance/s. It seems, then, that we are at an impasse. Adding to this issue is that the ending of Mark has always been hotly contested. Mark 16:9-20—where the reference to a "different form" is found—is missing from both the earliest manuscripts on record and certain early witnesses. Many translations indicate this prior to the start of the section. This does not mean we should discount it, but it does mean that we should not hinge a great deal on either interpretation. In the end, it could mean that Jesus was somewhat of a shape-shifter. It could also merely be a reference to his transformed resurrection body. We simply cannot be sure on this one.

Another interesting passage of relevance actually refers not to Jesus, but to the most unholy of entities: Satan. When Paul warned his faltering flock in Corinth about the many suspicious characters in their midst—asserting that some were even masquerading as apostles (2 Cor. 11:13)—he added the following comment: "No wonder, for even Satan disguises himself as an angel of light" (11:14). On its face, the comparison was not about literal appearances, but about the ulterior motives that both the false apostles and Satan shared in common. There is no doubt truth in that correlation. That said, it doesn't check all the boxes on this particular sheet. The word translated as "disguises" (*metaschēmatizō*) serves a very specific function within the New Testament. In fact, it is used only five times in total (all by Paul), and literally means "to change in fashion or appearance."[39] This means that when the fake apostles appeared to the

---

[39] Strong's Concordance, 3345: "metaschématizó."

people in Corinth (and elsewhere, we know) they did so not just in deed, but also in appearance. In some way, shape, or form, they were dressing to look more "apostle-like." Similarly, Satan changes both his outward and inward appearance to look more far more virtuous than he really is. The extent to which he can physically do so is unclear, but it seems as though it is possible. It is also worth mentioning that the first appearance of Satan in the Bible was in the form of a serpent (Gen. 3:1). Whether this meant that he literally became a serpent, or simply used a serpent to do his bidding, is heavily debated and is difficult to clearly answer. Moreover, it is contested whether this account is to be taken as historical narrative or more symbolically. In truth, early Genesis seems to blend both together quite seamlessly.

While being only anecdotal in nature, there is a long history of people who firmly believe that angels appeared to them in a relatable way. Paul mentioned that, by showing hospitality to others, "some have entertained angels without knowing it" (Heb. 13:2b). Numerous individuals have told me that a being appeared to them in the form of light or even as someone they once knew in order to communicate a message. On the very day my paternal grandfather passed away, both my mother and brother believe they saw him standing in a crowd of people at a local baseball game. That was of course impossible, since he had died right before the game took place! It is difficult to know what we should make of these types of sightings and experiences. Are they visions, or are heavenly beings somehow showing themselves in a form we could recognize? While we cannot know to a certainty, we can at least feel comfortable affirming that they are making themselves known to us in one way or another. However, and as I have pointed out elsewhere,[40] we should not always trust every being that reveals itself to us. It is certainly possible that demonic entities would be capable of entering our lives by appearing as deceased friends or relatives.

---

[40] See *The Death Myth*, 136-143 for more on how evil entities can masquerade as those who are close to us in order to wreak havoc.

Naturally, many theologians view every single physical appearance of God or the angels as a temporary manifestation. Do not be fooled here though: if the heavenly beings are able to alter their appearances in myriad ways, this would not lead to the conclusion that they are otherwise unembodied. Beyond certain *a priori* beliefs, there is no rational reason to assume that unembodied beings can appear in different forms and embodied beings cannot. This is like the view that God has to be immaterial in order to create a material world. It simply isn't a logical necessity. Besides, and as I have already described, these entities *only* ever appear in tangible form throughout the Bible. This would be true of both the angels and the Son of God.

Regardless of whether the heavenly beings are actually demonstrating the ability to shape-shift, we know for a certainty that they exist with the type of bodies that permit them to do things we cannot. As was discussed in the very first section of this chapter, Jesus and the angels both exhibited the ability to simply appear and disappear at will. Their bodies apparently provide them with the power to transition between our realm and heaven, almost as though they are simply stepping into another room. We are not capable of doing this in our present condition. In a very profound way, Jesus—in his resurrected form—showed the ability to pass through doors even though he could still be touched (Jn. 20:19-29). It is difficult to ignore the reality that heavenly beings are not bound by the same rules we are, but it is equally hard to deny that they have some type of physical makeup. Perhaps their unique bodies allow them to present themselves in ways that truly stretch the human mind. As the Bible describes our future, we will someday find out!

Chapter Two

Life in Heaven

In the first chapter, we looked very closely at the bodily nature of the heavenly beings. I realize this notion is not going to be well received by many of you who are reading this. A God who has some physical form is just, well, not "God" to a lot of us. The same applies to the angels. As Origen stated in his own unique way, if we can even begin to grasp anything about God, then He ceases to be God. Of course, it was God who explained Himself to us, both in word and through the Word (Jn.1:1). Based on how the Bible describes our Creator, and how God came to us in the man Jesus, it seems inescapable that physical existence is in some way a mark of our being made in God's image. As powerful as this realization can be, we have to wonder if this as far as we can go. Can we learn any more about, or probe any deeper into, the inner workings of the heavenly beings? What does it mean to be a "spirit" or to be "spiritual?" How are heavenly beings able to interact with us, and why aren't we able to see them much of the time? These questions (and more) are the target of this chapter of the book.

The Spirit of the Text

An overlooked, but often assumed, aspect in understanding our relationship to God's realm and the heavenly beings is what it means to be a "spirit," or a "spiritual" being. It should be relatively clear why this is such an important issue to consider. If spirits and spiritual things are intended to be understood as being wholly non-physical, it would affect everything we understand about how we communicate with or experience them. But should we directly equate the word "spirit" with the word "immaterial?" Are spirits and spiritual things best understood in this way, or did the biblical authors in fact intend something different? You might be surprised to learn that the answer to these questions is both yes *and* no. Spiritual things are sometimes seen but are, at other times, completely hidden from our sight.

Just like when the issues of "images" and "likenesses" were discussed, it is crucial here that we do at least a bit of research into the language employed by the biblical authors. Terms like "spirit" and "spiritual" are used a great many times throughout both the Old and New Testaments, so seeing these concepts through the eyes of those who authored the ancient texts is imperative. While this section will begin with a study into the most important terms we should understand, it will then segue into the eye-opening conclusions that can be drawn from them. In keeping with the order of the Bible and its progression, let's begin once more in the Old Testament.

To say that the term "spirit," or its variations, is used in diverse ways would be quite an understatement. In reality, the term can have about as many meanings as any biblical word we could wish to consider. The primary Hebrew word that is used in these instances is *ruach*, and it shows up hundreds of times throughout the OT.[41] To get an idea for just how disparately it is used, consider the following examples. Sometimes, the term *ruach* refers to one of life's most ordinary occurrences: the blowing of the wind. Consider Daniel 2:35 and 7:2, for instance. In both of these verses, Daniel used the term in this exact way. The first reference is used to describe one of King Nebuchadnezzar's dreams, in which the many metal parts of the statue are ground and blown away by the *wind* like a chaff of wheat (2:35). The second usage refers to a dream (or vision) that Daniel

---

[41] Strong's Concordance, 7307-8 "ruach."

himself had, in which he saw the "winds of heaven" stirring up the sea (7:2). The word *ruach* is also best translated this way in a text like Exodus 14:21, where God used the wind to part the waters of the Red Sea (or, the Sea of Reeds).

On close inspection, the book of Daniel provides somewhat of a crash course on the word *ruach*.[42] At one point, Nebuchadnezzar refers to the "spirit of the holy gods" (4:8), which is a mysterious expression that at least displays his belief that Daniel had a special connection to the heavenly world. There are much clearer examples of the term, however. It was said that Daniel had an "extraordinary spirit" (5:12). The conceited king, Nebuchadnezzar, fell when he came to possess a "spirit" of arrogance (5:20). As for Daniel, some of his visions even caused his "spirit" to become distressed and rattled (7:15). Clearly, those usages have nothing to do with an immaterial being, but with some faculty or emotion that physical human beings possess. This would be like saying, "he is full of himself," or "she has a gentle spirit." Of course, the terms associated with *ruach* appear many other places throughout the Old Testament. In Judges 8:3, for example, it is often interpreted as the word "anger." Many translations render Rahab's—when she had sheltered the Israelite spies—use of this term as "courage" (Jos. 2:11). Oddly, the term is also used to describes Job's bad "breath," which had even become offensive to his own wife (19:17). In truth, this is just a small sampling of the ways in which *ruach* appears.

In the NT, the word that is most frequently translated as "spirit" is the word *pneuma*. Like *ruach*, *pneuma* is generally translated in the following ways: wind, spirit, and rarely breath. John 3:8 illustrates both the former and the latter uses in one verse: "The *wind* blows where it wishes and you hear the sound of it, but do not know where it comes from and where it is going: so is everyone who is born of the *Spirit*." This shows the tremendous versatility of the term. While almost all the usages of *pneuma*

---

[42] See Daniel 4:8-9, 4:18, 5:11, 5:14.

can be translated as any of those three words, it is overwhelmingly translated as "spirit." When the attributive adjective "holy" is added, *pneuma* is taken to mean the third member of the Godhead, the Spirit.[43]

The term is also used in some very interesting ways: ways that are anything but expected. In particular, one of the variants of this term has some very surprising implications. Consider the following items: food and drink. None of us would *ever* describe these items as immaterial. Instead, we know that they are decidedly material in nature. This should sound peculiar, since they are repeatedly mentioned as being "spiritual" realities. That's right: food and drink are spiritual things. Hearkening back to the Israelites' time in the wilderness, Paul stated the following:

> "For I do not want you to be unaware, brethren, that our fathers were all under the cloud and all passed through the sea; and all were baptized into Moses in the cloud and in the sea; and all ate the same spiritual food; and all drank the same spiritual drink, for they were drinking from a spiritual rock which followed them; and the rock was Christ" (1 Cor. 10:1-4).

The "spiritual" food and drink Paul was referring to was the manna God provided (Ex. 16) and the water that sprang forth from the rock (Ex. 17:1-14). This was *real* food and drink, but its heavenly and miraculous origin elevated it to being "spiritual" food and drink. As I will later explain, even the bodies we will one day receive are described in this way.

This has been another important word lesson for all of us (myself included). Through the Hebrew term *ruach*, we saw that the Old Testament view of the "spirit" is extremely diverse. It can be used to talk about anything from the wind that blows to the courage that propels us, and many things in between. The OT does not have a word that specifically urges us to interpret it as being equivalent to "immaterial" or "incorporeal." It's simply not there. In truth, the NT doesn't contain a

---

[43] Strong's Concordance, 4151 "pneuma."

word of that nature, either. Now, that does not mean that *ruach* and *pneuma* cannot function in such a way at all. The meaning of both words is extremely contextual, and they most certainly do not *directly* translate to "immaterial." No one would suggest that our breath or the wind are material things in the normal sense of word. Of course, such things are products of material realities, and neither exist apart from them. This fact is actually part of my case for why something like a disembodied spirit is utter nonsense; we know of no immaterial thing that exists wholly apart from some type of physical substrate. Not one.

Believe it or not, we are beginning to get somewhere. You see, it is not just food, drink, or bodies that are characterized as being "spiritual." Songs—which are sung by tangible people—are said to be spiritual (Eph. 5:19, Col. 3:16). Thoughts and words—the product of tangible faculties—are likewise described in this way (1 Cor. 2:13). The same could be said of spiritual gifts (1 Cor. 12). Even the OT Law—which was physically recorded and applies to our physical actions—is described as spiritual (Rom. 7:14). Perhaps most importantly, people are frequently characterized throughout the New Testament with identical terminology. We—you and I—can be spiritual. Yet we are, of course, physical beings. It appears that the litmus test for being a mature Christian in the early church (and presumably, in our time as well) was both simple and strangely complex: is he or she a "spiritual" person? Now, you might equate this question with something like, does he or she "have the Spirit of God in them?" That, however, would be a false comparison. The NT is quite clear that *all* believers are blessed to receive God's Spirit: "The Spirit Himself testifies with our spirit that we are the children of God" (Rom. 8:16). There are a host of other examples that could be included here.[44] While having the Spirit of God in one's life is certainly essential in being a "spiritual" person, it is not all that is entailed. Even the new believer has been given assurance by the Spirit that he or she is a child of God.

---

[44] See Ephesians 1:13-14, 2 Corinthians 1:22, John 16:13, for a few of these examples.

Rather than trying to concoct some deeply theological explanation for what a "spiritual" person is, it would be best to allow the biblical authors to explain it. Paul once gave the following advice to the church in Galatia: "Brethren, even if anyone is caught in any trespass, you who are spiritual, restore such a one in a spirit of gentleness; each one looking to yourself, so that you too will not be tempted" (6:1). Those who are spiritual can help those who are not, by both calling them away from sin and helping them to leave it. Implicit in this is the view that spiritual people are not themselves entangled in sin. At another time, Paul wrote these words to his most rebellious church:

> "And I, brethren, could not speak to you as to spiritual men, but as to men of flesh, as to infants in Christ. I gave you milk to drink, not solid food; for you were not yet able to receive it. Indeed, even now you are not yet able, for you are still fleshly. For since there is jealousy and strife among you, are you not fleshly, and are you not walking like mere men?" (1 Cor. 3:1-3).

The analogy cannot be missed. Many of the believers in Corinth were like immature children: newborns who still needed to be fed by their mothers. They were nowhere near mature enough in their faith (i.e. they were not "spiritual" enough) to handle anything beyond the basics. This truth is no different today, as we all begin as infants in Christ. The problem is that some individuals choose to stay at that level. They are believers; they just aren't "spiritual."

If one does not ultimately mature in their faith, there is a high probability that they will lose it. This is probably why Paul revealed the following to the church at Colossae: ". . . we have not ceased to pray for you and to ask that you may be filled with the knowledge of His will in all spiritual wisdom and understanding" (1:9b). This wasn't ordinary wisdom of the world, but *spiritual wisdom*. Perhaps the best way to summarize this concept is to say that there are ultimately two types of human beings: earthly (or fleshly) and spiritual. The new believer is immature and straddles the line between being transformed into the image of Christ and behaving like fallen Adam. The spiritual believer has moved beyond this infancy stage and has reached another level. Fundamentally, this is what spiritual things are all about: reaching a higher level.

As it turns out, "spiritual things" either directly equate or apply to "material things." Food, drink, bodies, songs, laws, people, and more, are all discussed in this way throughout the Bible. Besides the assumption that we should directly compare something that is spiritual with something that is immaterial, the Bible itself doesn't really give us much reason to believe this. At this point, you are probably wondering if I am really saying what you think I am saying. The answer to that question is yes; I am really saying that "spirits" and "spiritual things" have been very misunderstood for a long time: not by everyone, but certainly by parts of the church at large. The biblical authors did not use the terms previously discussed to talk about items that have no substance or physicality. At least, they rarely did so. But as I said, even the exceptions—things like wind or breath—correspond and relate only to the material world; both are caused by material forces, and both are only understood in relation to the physical world. Perhaps it is time that we reevaluate how we view these issues; not because I said so, but because the biblical authors have.

Surely, I need to slow down with this "spiritual is inseparable from physical" rhetoric. I mean, to this point I have talked about "spiritual things" and how they relate to our world. We have established that human beings can be spiritual—as the Bible itself reveals—but what about the heavenly beings? How do these exact issues pertain to them? The Bible tells us about the Spirit of God, and that both angelic and demonic entities are spirits. But could it be possible that "spiritual beings" are not so very different from "spiritual things?" Strangely enough, there are even more reasons to believe that spiritual beings are also connected to material existence. Thus far, we have already begun to see that the Bible clearly points in this direction. As another step towards seeing this, we will need to take a closer look at something most of us deeply enjoy: eating.

The Jesus Diet

It seems like almost everyone today struggles with their weight. We fight calories, wrestle foods, and deprive ourselves of the things we really want to eat on nearly a daily basis. Over the last several decades, we have seen the emergence of the Atkins Diet, the Paleo Diet, the Keto Diet, the Dukan Diet, and about every other kind of diet imaginable. Some people have tried them all! By tomorrow, the next big dietary trend will probably be upon us. We also appeal to others for help with weight loss, like Jenny Craig, Weight Watchers, Nutrisystem, and the like. But why do we do it? Is it so we can feel better about ourselves? Is it so we can look better than those around us? Or, are we simply trying to equip ourselves to live a little longer, and to be a little healthier? These are certainly not bad reasons to worry about our weight. As anyone who is out of their early twenties can attest, fighting the scale can be a very real—and very difficult—war to undertake.

However, it is also an uphill battle: one that we will all lose sooner or later. Even the health and fitness nuts among us—with whom I do not belong—know that, at some point, one must accept that things like "thunder thighs" and "Dunlap Disease" are pretty much unavoidable. To some degree, at least. Mother Nature is still undefeated in this capacity. But what if I told you that it doesn't have to be this way? What if you could eat all the food you wanted, every single day of the week, and never gain any weight whatsoever? I mean it: not a single ounce! Before you get too excited, there is one rather significant catch. You can indeed satisfy every eating desire that my ever arise. However, you must be Jesus himself, or at least possess a resurrection body like his.

Undoubtedly, I need to explain myself a bit here. Just know in advance that my dietary introduction is nowhere near as strange as the reasons why I wrote it. It is extremely difficult to articulate how far some thinkers—of both the past and present—will go in their efforts to ensure that both God and the angels continue to be viewed as incorporeal beings. In one of the absolute strangest perspectives I have ever read on *any* topic, I recall Thomas Aquinas' view of when the resurrected Jesus dined with his disciples. After Jesus had been raised from the dead and given the very first of the resurrection (or "spiritual," as Paul called them) bodies, it is recorded that he ate a piece of fish in the presence of the apostles. After the initial shock of seeing Jesus physically appear to them, Luke tells of what happened next:

> "While they still could not believe it because of their joy and amazement, He said to them, 'Have you anything here to eat?' They gave him a piece of a broiled fish; and he took it and ate it before them" (24:41-43).

Now, normal people would read this passage and think that Jesus met with his apostles, that he asked them for something to eat, and that he went on to devour a piece of fish. But that's why we are normal people, I suppose. You see, it takes a historically great theologian to extract the "real meaning" behind this text, and to interpret this event as it *really* occurred. This would take someone like the immortal Thomas Aquinas, probably. Fortunately for us, Aquinas actually did write about this event. Here is how he saw it:

> ". . . some cases are true only with the truth of signification, as the eating ascribed to an angel, because an angel does not have the organs for eating. But what is signified by their eating is true, that is, the desire they have for our salvation. But Christ's act of eating after the resurrection was true both with the truth of signification, because he did it to show that he had a human nature, which he did in truth have, and his eating was true according to its species, because he had the organs used for eating. However, the effects consequent on eating were not present, since the food was not transformed into his substance, since he had a glorified and incorruptible body. It was dissolved into pre-existing matter by the divine power."[45]

Disregarding Aquinas' standard way of writing—which is at least partially intended to elude the "peasantry"—the thought here is still discernible. Though Jesus "ate" the fish in the presence of the disciples, he did not actually eat it. Not really. It certainly looked like he devoured it, as any person with a "human nature" (in Aquinas' words) would have, but somewhere between his illusory mouth and his non-existent stomach, the food magically vanished. In essence, it was just a good show. This view is extremely problematic. The central purpose of Jesus eating the fish was so he could prove that he was a physical person, rather than some type of apparition. To put it more succinctly, Jesus was supposed to be showing them that he is the kind of entity that can actually eat. That being the case, what is the point of making that gesture if the entire ordeal was some type of deception? Would that not defeat the entire purpose? I mean, why not simply tell them that heavenly beings have no need of eating? None of it adds up.

As you would expect, many others have written similar things. John Calvin went a step farther, saying:

> "And, indeed, though he has obtained a new and heavenly life, and has no more need of meat and drink than angels have, still he voluntarily condescends to join in the common usages of mortals. During the whole course of his life, he had subjected himself to the necessity of eating and drinking; and now, though relieved from that necessity, he eats for the purpose of convincing his disciples of the certainty of his resurrection."[46]

While we are on the topic, I simply have to confess something: I rather enjoy eating and drinking. In fact, I think these are two of the most pleasurable aspects of human existence; they are truly gifts from God. Don't you agree? You don't have to be a "foodie" to understand the

---

[45] Thomas Aquinas, "Commentary on John 21," Lecture 2, 2612.
[46] John Calvin, *Calvin's Commentary on the Bible: Luke 24.*

simple pleasures of having a great meal. But in the gospel according to John Calvin, Jesus was "relieved" of that "necessity." I thought the same thing the last time I ate a good piece of fish; "Praise God that's done and over with . . . I can't wait until I never have to do that again!" In all seriousness, Calvin was saying that both Jesus and the angels do not *truly* eat. Jesus "subjected himself" to doing it for our sake, but it was unnecessary for him. Essentially, it was another display; none of the heavenly beings regularly eat, and they certainly do not need to.

Contrary to that thinking, Jesus was not the only heavenly being to eat with mere mortals. Prior to God's destruction of Sodom, two angels appeared to warn Lot (Abraham's nephew) and his family about the coming disaster:

> "Now the two angels came to Sodom in the evening as Lot was sitting in the gate of Sodom. When Lot saw them, he rose to meet them and bowed down with his face to the ground. And he said, 'Now behold, my lords, please turn aside into your servant's house, and spend the night, and wash your feet; then you may rise early and go on your way'" (Gen. 19:1-2).

First, notice that the angels appeared completely embodied (recall the foot washing remark). In an extremely perverted turn of events, scores of men from Sodom later surrounded Lot's house, demanding that Lot release the angels so they can "have relations with them" (Gen. 19:4-5). They looked human-like, but were obviously a bit out of the ordinary in appearance. Why else would they flock to those two "men" above the other possible options? I will discuss this again later in the book.

Before the men of Sodom came, however, Genesis reveals something that is odd for a totally different reason (thankfully). After Lot persuaded the angels to stay with him, ". . . they turned aside to him and entered his house; and he prepared a feast for them, and baked unleavened bread, and they ate" (19:3). Just as the resurrected Jesus did centuries later, the two angels visiting Lot ate real food in the presence of human beings. Let us not forget Jesus' words after the institution of the Lord's Supper: "But I say to you, I will not drink of this fruit of the vine from now on until the day when I drink it new with you in My Father's kingdom" (Mt. 26:29). The symbolic significance of this statement can only go so far; clearly, Jesus was telling them that he would indeed drink wine again when he returned.

There are other references to consider as well. Psalm 78 declares that the manna God graciously provided for the Israelites in the Wilderness was actually the "bread of angels" (vv. 24-25). Then there was the meal that Abraham served to his three angelic visitors, prior to the discovery that he and Sarah would have a child: "He took curds and milk and the calf which he had prepared, and placed *it* before them; and he was standing by them under the tree as they ate" (Gen. 18:8). Moreover, the book of Revelation speaks of a day when Jesus will return to earth—a day when the King would return with his Kingdom. What would be more proper to celebrate the King's return than a feast (Rev. 19:6-9)? I know, I know: all of these references are also completely figurative. It is recorded that Jesus ate, and that we will all eat and drink together when he returns. Being that we will all have glorious new bodies at that point, I wonder: will we just be eating to prove the "certainty of our resurrections" to one another? Doesn't it seem more likely that partaking in food and drink will still be a feature of our existence in the new heavens and new earth?

It is typically taught that these examples should be dismissed as being either totally allegorical or simply misinterpreted. The eating exhibitions of the angels and the risen Jesus—along with their physical appearances in general—were no doubt "shows" that were intended to make everyone think that heavenly beings have bodies and that they can even eat. If we are being honest about what the Bible is telling us, these explanations strain credibility. At some point, we should all wonder if these attempts to subvert the plain reading of the texts should be accepted. While there are not scores of examples to point to where heavenly beings sat down to dine, there is certainly a known biblical precedent for it. Further, there are zero examples where the text so much as implies that the eating wasn't real, or that the heavenly beings did so without bodies. The evidence we have in hand obviously suggests that heavenly beings eat and drink. At the very least, it tells us they are capable of such things.

While I will later discuss other amazing feats of theological acrobatics, the miraculous "Jesus diet" provides further insight on a very important topic. The issue is that both God and the angels are very staunchly—almost obsessively, really—viewed as incorporeal entities. I say "obsessively" in light of views like the ones offered by Calvin, Aquinas, and a slew of others that I will continue to mention. Eating and drinking would necessitate a being that is truly tangible in nature, rather than one who is simply manifesting (temporarily appearing, really) as such. This is a step that most theologians simply aren't willing to take. The fact that God and the angels are referred to as "spirits" or "spiritual beings" has, for some reason, assured most thinkers that they do not possess bodies or have any physical substance to them at all. However, we have already seen many places where the biblical authors applied this terminology to things like food, drink, bodies, and even people. As we continue, I hope this will become more apparent. The truth is that there is very little reason to hold that a "spirit"—in the way the Bible typically uses the term—is an immaterial being at all.

Unseen Forces

"Now to the King eternal, immortal, invisible, the only God, be honor and glory forever and ever. Amen."[47]

The view that the heavenly beings are unembodied, incorporeal, and immaterial is about as widespread as the belief that each of us possesses (or is, really) a soul that will one day live apart from the body. Of course, many people believe that Satan lives in hell, and that Jesus was always

---

[47] 1 Tim. 1:17

one big bundle of joy to everyone he came in contact with. These are just a couple of the unfounded beliefs that are common within the church. When we put the last few sections of the book together, we are forced to ask another critical question about the heavenly beings: why are they typically unseen? Is it because they are immaterial after all, or is there another explanation? To answer this, we must take an even closer look at how the Bible describes both God and the angels. First, we will examine the angelic beings.

As I have suggested, it is typically taught that angels are incorporeal. Well known author, J. Warner Wallace, described this very clearly when he said,

> "Angels are immaterial, spiritual beings. But when they appear to humans, they typically take on our form. Why would they do this? Perhaps it is because they love us and want to connect with us as created beings."[48]

Not only does Wallace assert that angels are immaterial beings, he also essentially equates "spiritual" with "immaterial." Aquinas—following his own obsession with immaterial realms and beings—reemerges to show his agreement: "Consequently, since the angels are not bodies, nor have they bodies naturally united with them, as is clear from what has been said (Article 1; I:50:1), it follows that they sometimes assume bodies."[49] Naturally, one good assumption deserves another. Indeed, angels are not *really* embodied beings; they only appear to be on occasion.

To this point, I have suggested that the Bible does not contrast physical things with spiritual things, as though the two are opposites. It is imperative to mention that a "physical" mindset—meaning "worldly"—is often contrasted with a "spiritual" mindset (particularly in 1 Corinthians), but the Bible does not equate "spiritual" items/beings with "immaterial" items/beings. By now, this should be obvious because physical things are

---

[48] J. Warner Wallace, "Why Did God Create Angelic Beings?"
[49] Thomas Aquinas. *The Summa Theologica*, 1:51:2.

often characterized as being "spiritual." Most recently—and at points here and there—I have gone a step further and proposed an idea that no doubt seems absurd to many readers: that even the heavenly beings have some type of tangible existence. But if a spirit is not an immaterial being, what is it? We know that God, the angels, and the demons, are all three referred to as "spirits." It is also true that we are often unable to see these beings with the naked eye, and that they can affect us without being visible. It is always best to start with what we do know, and work our way out from there.

Hebrews 1:14 refers to angels as "ministering spirits" (*leitourgika pneumata*), and the rest of the Bible often notes that the angels work in this capacity.[50] More often, demons are referred to as evil or "unclean" spirits. The NT is replete with events of possession, in which unseen demons had taken control over unfortunate human victims. As I have chronicled elsewhere, Jesus actually became famous (at least, at first) as an exorcist, and the first portion of Mark's gospel seems to be aimed at making sure that we initially think of Jesus in this way.[51] After the Resurrection, Jesus referenced the fact that a "spirit" does not have flesh and bones (Lk. 24:39), as he most certainly did. That is a point of its own, because this verse also makes clear the fact that the resurrected Jesus was a glorified being of flesh and bone: a view that some classical Christian thinkers deny, if not outright reject as heresy. If a "spirit" (in this context) does not have flesh and bones, it clearly means that Jesus did. We cannot have it both ways.

However, we also have to be honest enough to admit what Jesus was saying to his apostles in that moment—while he stood before them as a physical being, a spirit could not have. The obvious conclusion is that the word spirit (*pneuma*) can, *at times*, be used to reference an entity without

---

[50] For a few examples, consider the angelic visitors that warned Lot and his family prior to the destruction of Sodom and Gomorrah (Gen. 19:1-22), as well as the angels that ministered to both Jesus and Paul (Mt. 4:11, Acts 27:23-26).
[51] For more information on this issue, refer to *The Death Myth*, 78-84.

physical form: an unembodied being, so to speak. To think otherwise would require that we twist Jesus' words, which is something none of us should be willing to do. The curious thing is that the other synoptic gospels—the gospels that are known to share a great many similarities—use a different (and unusual) term to describe a similar event. Both Matthew and Mark record that the apostles thought they had seen a "ghost" (*phantasma*) when they witnessed Jesus walking on the sea (Mt. 14:26, Mk. 6:49). Obviously, they felt as though only some type of unembodied entity could walk on water. I have two reasons for comparing these events and the terminology used to describe them. The first is that both occurrences prove that the word "spirit" *can* function to describe an immaterial entity. The word "spirit" can work like the word "ghost," though the latter is only used twice throughout the entire New Testament. I have more to say about this later in the section.

The second point is a bit more crucial within the scope of the present topic, and it is that the previous events also show that immaterial ghosts and spirits do not really exist. If you think about it, neither the apostles' belief that Jesus was a ghost nor Jesus' statement that spirits do not have flesh and bones leads us to believe that either are real. The apostles thought Jesus was a ghost because of the extreme nature of the events. This is no different than if you came upon a horrified individual and said, "you look like you've seen a ghost!" This was most likely intended to be a figure of speech rather than a statement that they subscribed to the existence of ghosts. Nothing else in the Bible would really mesh with such a view, particularly the standard Jewish belief system that they almost certainly adhered to. Jesus' statement does not tell us that he believed in immaterial specters, either. One can certainly smell the sarcasm written all over Jesus' words there, when the apostles doubted that they were really seeing a risen, embodied Savior; ". . . a spirit does not have flesh and bones as you see that I have." You stubborn apostles—what were you thinking?

Though the term "spirit" was used—and very rarely, at that—to refer to immaterial beings, these occasions were intended to function as contrasts to reality. Jesus was embodied (not a "ghost") when they saw him walking on the water, and he was embodied (not a "spirit") when they encountered him after the Resurrection. If anything, these events actually disprove the existence of disembodied spirits. To add further evidence to the case, consider that spiritism, divination, necromancy, and the like, are strictly forbidden in the Bible.[52] God's people are cautioned again and again about trying to contact the deceased or beings that exist beyond this world. If the spirits of the dead do indeed exist, there is no logical reason to ban believers from attempting to communicate with them. The reason it is forbidden is that unholy entities are contacted by these efforts, which is why all forms of spiritism and divination take on an evil connotation within the Bible. Not only is there little talk about incorporeal entities within Scripture, we are clearly warned about such a prospect.

This is a suitable place to apply the brakes for a moment and return to something that has come up a couple of times already:[53] the issue of the "spiritual body." Think about this expression. On the face of it, the two terms do not appear to go together. In fact, some may see these terms as polar opposites. A body can be physical *and* spiritual, at the same time? When we take off the lenses of two thousand years of philosophical speculation and "this is how it is!" church instruction, we discover that the two words are in fact not opposite at all. You might even say that they can be complementary.

In actuality, the term "spiritual" was being used to describe the resurrection *body*! But there is something far more telling that Paul reveals in 1 Corinthians 15. In his evaluation of both Adam and Jesus, consider one of Paul's points of contrast: "So it is written: 'The first man Adam

---

[52] For evidence of this fact, see Lev. 19:31, 20:6; Dt. 18:10-12; 1 Sam. 28:3; and Acts 16:16.
[53] Refer back to the section entitled, "Different Forms?"

became a living being'; the last Adam, a life-giving spirit" (15:45, NIV). To clarify, the "last Adam" was undoubtedly a reference to Jesus. The entire passage makes this obvious, as do Paul's statements elsewhere (Rom. 5, especially). That being the case, it is clear that Paul referred to Jesus as a "life-giving spirit." Jesus is a spirit? How can that be? The first step in understanding this apparent conundrum is to again affirm that this entire paradigm needs to be reconsidered. Jesus returned from the dead with a transformed body, appeared in physical form to hundreds of people (at least), ate and drank with his apostles, and was touched by several of them. All the while he was also described as a "spirit." This speaks volumes. Either the Bible is sharply contradicting itself on these matters, or we have long misunderstood what spiritual things really are. Personally, I am placing my bets on the latter.

With this said, the central point is that the term "spirit" is very seldom used to describe something that is immaterial. More than that, it was almost always used differently. The truth is that the Bible describes spirits as entities that exist in a more advanced way than us; they exist on a higher plane or level of being, if you will. As one rather popular dictionary defines the term, a spirit is a "supernatural being or essence."[54] Primarily, a spirit is a heavenly being of greater power, ability, standing, and overall existence. This is akin to the difference between ordinary food, drink, bodies, and people, and *spiritual* food, drink, bodies, and people. These items do not cease to be tangible because they are also "spiritual." Recall the previous discussion concerning what it means to be a spiritual person. This has absolutely nothing—nothing whatsoever—to do with leaving our bodies and all of material existence. Instead, it has everything to do with moving to Christian maturity, and doing so within a tangible world. Moreover, beings (angels) that are said to be "spirits" are the same as the entities that physically appear to people (and even eat) all throughout the

---

[54] Merriam-Webster, "spirit."

Bible. Jesus himself clearly had a resurrection body, but was also described as a "life-giving spirit."

That is all well and good. *Perhaps* the angelic beings actually possess bodies and a physical existence. Maybe they are not unseen because they lack all substance. Even if that is true, we still need to apply these matters to God. How do we make sense of things, since God is so assuredly detached from physical existence? We "know" this to be the case for several reasons. It would necessarily take an immaterial being to create a physical world, as essentially all arguments from *First Cause* assert.[55] It would take an incorporeal being to manifest in various ways, or to remain unseen. Most of all, we know that God is unembodied because the Bible tells us so. Both the Old and New Testaments are absolutely clear that God is an immaterial being. But is that true?

While I have already touched upon the issue of God's embodiment, this is an ideal time to bring the matter back into the discussion. The issue of what it means to be "spirit" and to be unseen has particular importance concerning how we understand God. The truth is, the Bible nowhere refers to God as an immaterial being. Not in one single place. We already know that Jesus has a resurrection body, and most theologians are more than happy to tell us that the Son (or, the "pre-incarnate Christ") appears in physical form throughout the Old Testament.[56] But what about the Father? God the Father is immaterial, right? When we consult the Bible itself, it answers this question with a resounding *no*. In fact—and I say this quite honestly—almost every single time I have read that God (the

---

[55] Arguments from *First Cause* vary in numerous ways, but they share in common the belief that, in order for our universe (or any material universe) to have come into being, there must have been something that is not reducible to material causes that initiated it. Since we cannot have material causes giving rise to material causes infinitely into the past, there must be an immaterial cause behind it all. That immaterial cause is argued to be God.

[56] I refer you to Tim Chaffer's article, *Theophanies in the Old Testament.* This explains some of the issues surrounding "the angel of the Lord," and discusses why most people believe the pre-incarnate Christ (Christ before he was made flesh) appeared in bodily form throughout the OT.

Father) is incorporeal, John 4:24 is the only piece of biblical evidence that is brought forward. I urge you to do your own study (outside of this book) on what it means to be made in God's image. If you do, I believe you will find that John 4:24 is virtually the only verse of Scripture that is ever used to show that God is unembodied. I have no doubt that it has already come to mind for many readers before now. It's just so obvious, isn't it? "God is spirit, and those who worship Him must worship in spirit and truth." If you noticed, I included the entire verse here. If we didn't know any better, we would think—based on the way it is used—that the phrase "God is spirit" is all that is involved. It is actually the second part of the verse that should cause us to rethink its intended meaning, and I will get to that momentarily. But let's begin with the first part: 4:24a, if you will. It is extremely important to point out that the verse does not read, "God is *a* spirit," but "God is spirit."

In the original texts, there is no article associated with the term *pneuma*. It is wrong to place "a" in front of the term "spirit." This essentially means that the term "spirit" is being used to describe a feature of God's existence; this is not trying to tell us about *how* God exists (as a "spirit"), but is trying to tell us a characteristic about Him (He *is* "spirit"). I am not trying to pull some interpretive trick here, and fool people who have not studied the Greek language. Our English translations have rendered this verse correctly (so long as they do not add the "a"). I'm just not sure that we have interpreted it correctly. Based on our findings about what a spirit is in the biblical sense, even if it read, "God is *a* spirit," it still would not directly tell us that He is unembodied. It could mean that, but would likely not. The fact that the verse actually reads "God is spirit" essentially slams the door on that particular interpretation.

If John 4:24 is not telling us that the Father exists without a tangible body, what is it telling us? This is where the second part of the verse—which is almost always ignored—can help to shed some light on the issue. That part reads, ". . . those who worship Him must worship in spirit and truth." Notice that the word spirit (*pneuma*) is used in this part of the verse as well. This time, it is applied to the way we are supposed to worship God. It seems only reasonable, and contextually forthright, to interpret this term the same way in both instances. This is where it gets interesting. If the first usage is supposed to tell us that God is an immaterial being, then the second usage needs to be interpreted in the same way; we must worship God as immaterial beings, or with the immaterial spirit inside of our bodies. God is immaterial, and we must worship Him in that way. That could be a problem, since we are physical beings!

Notice something else about this verse: the description "in spirit" sounds eerily like something else we read in Scripture, does it not? I recall the words of John, as recorded in Revelation: "I was *in the Spirit* on the Lord's day, and I heard behind me a loud voice like *the sound* of a trumpet . . ." (1:10). The same expression is used again in 4:2. It's interesting that John is traditionally held to have written both the Gospel of John and Revelation, and both texts include statements about being "in (the) Spirit" or "in spirit." In the original language, both read the same: *en pneumati*. I would suggest that the words we read in John 4:24 should be interpreted in much the same way as those in Revelation. Being "in (the) Spirit" or worshipping "in spirit" are both expressions that imply we are experiencing a heightened sense of reality. For lack of a better way to say it, we are "plugged in" to God's system. Jesus expressed this reality when the Pharisees said they believed that the Messiah would be the son of David:

> "He said to them, 'Then how does David *in the Spirit* call Him 'Lord,' saying, The Lord said to my Lord, 'Sit at my right hand, until I put your enemies beneath your feet.' 'If David then calls Him 'Lord,' how is He his son?"[57]

When David was in a heightened sense of awareness through the Spirit, he was able to understand long ago that the Messiah would actually be his "Lord," rather than his son or one simply coming in his family line. Worshiping "in spirit" means that we are worshipping through the Spirit

---

[57] Mt. 22:43-45, emphasis mine.

on a higher level, in all truth and sincerity. It does not mean we are worshipping with some immaterial being inside of us, or as unembodied entities.

Now, recall the earlier discussion about the nature of spiritual things. The most fundamental way of understanding a spirit or a spiritual thing from a biblical standpoint is that both are advanced and elevated beyond more earthly, mundane items or beings. Spiritual food, drink, bodies, worship, people, etc., are of a higher quality than they are in the typical sense. I believe this is exactly what John 4:24 is telling us. God is a higher-level, heavenly being, and we must worship Him as such. In plainest terms, the verse is telling us that God demands the best worship possible. We must worship Him *in spirit*—in a pure and elevated manner— because He *is spirit*—a being of a pure and elevated existence. This interpretation not only fits with the rest of Scripture, but definitely fits the context of that situation. A Samaritan woman—who would have been considered to be a deplorable individual by most Jewish believers of the day—told Jesus that the Jews insisted on a particular kind of worship: an earthly, ritualistic variety that must take place at a certain location (the temple). Jesus' response was that God exists in a way that transcends our normal human traditions, and that He must be worshipped in an equally suitable way. True believers will worship God with all they have, and in the sincerest way possible. They will not have go to one particular building in order to accomplish a very specific set of tasks. They will not worship as immaterial spirits, either.

This bring us to another truly important thing to consider about John 4:24, and it involves the nature of the Holy Spirit in general. Consider this question: why is the Spirit called "the Spirit" to begin with? Why does the Bible consistently refer to the third person of the Godhead (or the Trinity, if you like) with that particular title? To be sure, this has been an enigmatic issue since the inception of the church, and probably well before that (this is even an issue within the OT). To put it plainly, the church has always had a much more difficult time making sense of the

Holy Spirit than either the Father or the Son. As I have described, it is widely believed that the biblical authors utilized the title "Spirit" to connote an unembodied and formless entity. We can be sure of this because John 4:24 is so often used to suggest that the Father—who is specifically mentioned as the subject of the conversation (4:21-23)—is incorporeal: "God is spirit." Frequently, there is a jump from this verse to Jesus' statement in Luke 24:39: "a spirit does not have flesh and bones as you see that I have." The alleged connection is that Jesus was telling the apostles that spirits are unembodied beings, so John 4:24 must be trying to say the same about God.

When you put these two verses (John 4:24 and Luke 24:39) together, you essentially have the entire case that is typically used to argue for an incorporeal God. As I described in detail, I have doubts that Jesus was subscribing to the belief in unembodied spirits (called "ghosts" in Mark and Matthew) to begin with. Like when the apostles saw Jesus walking on the sea (Mt. 14:26, Mk. 6:49), they were stunned to witness him appear before them in Luke 24:39. They thought they must have been seeing an apparition, because Jesus was supposed to be dead. This would be a very natural reaction for any of us, would it not? Imagine what you would think if a deceased friend appeared to you from nowhere, or you saw someone walking across a body of water. As I mentioned earlier, human beings don't do these things! The allusions to spirits or ghosts functioned more as rhetorical devices: figures of speech, if you will. With that said, these verses hardly qualify as Jesus telling us that immaterial entities exist and that they roam the earth. Luke 24:39 certainly does display an occasion where the word "spirit" is used to describe incorporeal beings, but even here it should not be interpreted as a literal description of reality.

In any event, some will persist in taking all this to mean that the Spirit of God is unembodied and has no tangible form whatsoever. However, consider the implications of this view. If "Spirit" is supposed to indicate this, then it must also indicate that the other two members of the

Godhead—the Father and the Son— are *not* unembodied and formless. In other words, they have bodies. The text would have to result in this conclusion. Otherwise, the title "Spirit" would be arbitrary and meaningless. Imagine the logic at play: the Spirit of God carries that name because He is unembodied . . . but the Father—if not even the Son—is also unembodied. Of what use would the title be? Why designate the Spirit in such a way? It simply wouldn't make sense to hold to this explanation.

On the other hand, let's imagine that something else is intended in calling the Spirit by that name: something that does not imply a lack of form or physicality. For instance, perhaps the Spirit is called that because of the way in which He interacts with us. If you recall, I mentioned that the word we sometimes translate as "Spirit/spirit" can also mean "wind" or "breath." With that in mind, we could say that the Spirit acts (according to our perception, at least) in a similar way to the wind. We cannot see, touch, smell or taste the Spirit of God. We know the Spirit when He "comes upon us;" we feel the divine presence. None of this would necessarily mean that the Spirit is unembodied. As I will discuss momentarily, this would simply mean that the Spirit is unseen or invisible to us. The major point of this section has been to show that, as far as Scripture is concerned, spirits and spiritual things do not run counter to form or materiality.

I recall what Tertullian once said, when considering the "spiritual" nature of God. In *Against Praxeas*—a thinker who believed that God has no tangible qualities—he wrote the following:

"How could it be, that He Himself is nothing, without whom nothing was made? How could He who is empty have made things which are solid, and He who is void have made things which are full, and He who is incorporeal have made things which have body? For although a thing may sometimes be made different from him by whom it is made, yet nothing can be made by that which is a void and empty thing. Is that Word of God, then, a void and empty thing, which is called the Son, who Himself is designated God? *'The Word was with God, and the Word was God.'* (John 1:1) It is written, *You shall not take God's name in vain.* (Exodus 20:7) This for certain is He *'who, being in the form of God, thought it not robbery to be equal with God.'* (Philippians 2:6) In what form of God? Of course he means in some form, not in none. For who will deny that God is a body, although *'God is a Spirit?'* (John 4:24) For Spirit has a bodily substance of its own kind, in its own form. Now, even if invisible things, whatsoever they be, have both their substance and their form in God, whereby they are visible to God alone, how much more shall that which has been sent forth from His substance not be without substance!"[58]

While there are several significant statements here, one stands out in particular: "For Spirit has a bodily substance of its own kind, in its own form." While I do not always agree with Tertullian's perspectives, the view expressed here is totally correct.

His case is strengthened when we look at Luke's account of Jesus' baptism. Here, we come across something truly mind-blowing. Luke recorded that the Holy Spirit "descended upon Him *in bodily form* like a dove" (3:22, my emphasis). Nearly all interpreters acknowledge the peculiarity of this statement. The word used there for "bodily" (*sómatikos*) is used only twice in the entire NT, and never again by Luke. The only other usage is in 1 Timothy 4:8, which says that ". . . bodily discipline is only of little profit, but godliness is profitable for all things, since it holds promise for the present life and also for the life to come." This is probably referencing an earlier verse (4:3), which reveals that false teachers were instructing believers not to marry and to abstain from certain foods. When you connect the dots, there is no denying that both uses of *sómatikos* are describing tangible bodies. This means that the Spirit's appearance at Jesus' baptism was corporeal. The text, then, is not telling us that the Spirit

---

[58] See *Against Praxeas,* Chapter 7.

literally became a dove and descended upon Jesus. Rather, it is telling us that the Spirit descended *in the manner* that a dove would: hovering, then resting.[59] Like Tertullian, I am not claiming that the Father, the Son, the Spirit, or even the angels, have the same exact type of bodies that we do; I am simply claiming that they have bodies *of some sort.*

There is a critical part of all this that still needs to be answered though: how do we explain the fact that heavenly beings are often unseen? In some sense, this question has already been answered. Paul's statements in Colossians 1:15-20 and 1 Timothy 1:17 reveal that God is invisible. The same principle was apparent when the group of angels appeared to Elisha and his servant (2 Ki. 6:17), when angels appeared from nowhere in Luke 2, and the other places mentioned. The point made in chapter one—that heaven is a realm, and that heavenly beings can pass between the two realms at will—shows us exactly how something can be "invisible," without being "immaterial" or "incorporeal." *Not being seen* is not the same as *not having physical form.* Along with this, I have provided many examples from Scripture where both God and the angels are clearly described in tangible terms.

To succinctly summarize the discussion, I am suggesting that there are two realistic ways to view unseen forces. The first is to see them as immaterial and having no physical form or substance at all. There is nothing "there," so to speak. Thus far, I have made the case that this view of unseen entities cannot account for the biblical information we have about the heavenly beings, and that it does not correspond with anything we understand about reality. Option two is almost entirely the opposite of the first: unseen forces are *not* immaterial, unembodied, disembodied, spaceless, formless, incorporeal, or anything of the sort. Instead, unseen forces are simply *invisible* forces. They indeed have form, occupy space, possess physicality, and so forth; it's just that we don't always see them. Of course, sometimes we actually do!

---

[59] *Elliot's Commentary: Luke 3:22.*

The opening verses of the Apostle Paul's immortal "hymn" reads as follows:

> "He is the image of the invisible God, the firstborn of all creation. For by Him all things were created, *both* in the heavens and on earth, visible and invisible, whether thrones or dominions or rulers or authorities—all things have been created through Him and for Him."[60]

If you recall the introduction to this section, God was referred to as "invisible" in 1 Timothy 1:17 as well. The world of the Bible is one of great mystery. The biblical authors understood that there are forces which completely transcend our normal comprehension. Some of them (no, not all) were given insight that enabled them to understand that there was another realm that both intersects and occurs separately from our own. They could not always see this realm, or the beings within it. However, they knew this world often made itself known in ours. *This* is the realm that Jesus seamlessly slipped in and out of. In this, we learn that "unseen" does not equate to "immaterial" any more than "spiritual" does. It does not for God, the angels, or even the heavenly realm they occupy. Rather—as the Bible explains reality—the word "unseen" seems to equate to "invisible." There is another world going on all around us, and in our midst. This is a tangible world with physical beings. Though we do not see this world (and its inhabitants) most of the time, we certainly feel its presence in our lives. One day, we will both see and experience the beings who currently live in this invisible world. In fact—as I will discuss in chapter four—we will even live with these heavenly beings.

---

[60] Colossians 1:15-16.

Time and Space

In addition to the previous reasons that lend credence to the idea that God, the angels, and the heavenly realm exist in some tangible way, we also have to consider the issues of time and space. Both concepts turn out to be connected. Concerning the latter, a truly immaterial entity would occupy no space whatsoever: such a being would not be spatially extended, so to speak. Of course, this is exactly how most theologians—*after* the first few centuries of church history—have viewed God. God has no spatial location. We could not rightly say that God exists "here," "there," or at any one place. Instead, God transcends all time and space, and is "omnipresent" (existing in all places simultaneously, without restriction). In his review of Paul Helm's book, *Eternal God*, William Lane Craig points this out for us, saying:

> "The biblical writers consistently *speak* of God as in time, but, Helm quite correctly points out, they with equal consistency speak of God as in space, too, and yet the vast majority of theologians and philosophers do not construe divine omnipresence as God's being spatially extended, but consider Him as transcending space."[61]

Craig is correct in saying that most theologians and philosophers feel as though God transcends time and space. This would mean that locations do not *truly* apply to God.

However, there is something perhaps more important to notice here. Both Craig and Helm acknowledge that most theologians and philosophers understand that the biblical authors spoke of God as existing in both time and space. That is, the Bible tells us—and, as we will see, very consistently—that God exists in real time and in a specific location at any given moment. God is not "outside of time," nor

---

[61] William Lane Craig, "A Review of Paul Helm's *Eternal God.*"

does He exist in all locations simultaneously. At least, *not as the Bible describes things.* It should come as no surprise that the Bible has one take on these issues, while our prestigious religious scholars view them in precisely the opposite way. Again, we are not talking about a subtle variation on what the Bible suggests, but a complete reversal. As I will continue to show—and as we have already seen in numerous ways—flipping Scripture upside down is just common practice for some of the church's "deepest thinkers." This is an unfortunate reality that began to occur almost at the instant the church began.

If that is true, what does the Bible really say about this issue? First off, the very existence of the heavens or the heavenly realm tells us that both God and the angels exist *somewhere.* More than that, they primarily exist in a different place than our planet or even our universe. Their "home base," if you will, is not here with us. I already addressed the existence of the heavenly realm at the onset of the book, so please revisit that if you need a refresher. Jesus' statement at the start of the Lord's Prayer tells us that the Father exists in heaven: "Our Father who is in heaven . . ." (Mt. 6:9). Note that Jesus did not say, "Our Father who is everywhere," or "Our Father who is here on earth." The Father exists *in heaven*, which immediately designates a location.

Everything else we read about God is consistent with this description. Jesus constantly told his followers that he had been "sent" from the Father, and that he would "return" to Him after the Resurrection. Jesus said, "He who receives you receives Me, and he who receives Me receives Him who sent Me" (Mt. 10:40). Mark's gospel records that Jesus said, "Whoever receives one child like this in My name receives Me; and whoever receives Me does not receive Me, but Him who sent Me" (9:37). I could go on with many other examples from Jesus, but this type of "sent" language exists all throughout the Bible.[62] Of course, Jesus was not the only person within the Trinity to be "sent" from heaven. Jesus instructed his apostles that after he left, another would come: "But the Helper, the Holy Spirit, whom the Father will send in My name, He will teach you all things, and bring to your remembrance all that I said to you" (Jn. 14:26). This, too, is a consistent theme.[63]

The pattern of sending others from one place to another involves the non-divine players in the biblical narrative as well. Throughout the entire Bible, angels are sent from God to speak to humans. Both the Hebrew and Greek terms we translate as "angel" (*malak* and *aggelos*) essentially mean "messenger." That is, someone who takes something from one place to another. In this case, angels carry information from God in the heavenly realm to us on earth. The word "apostle" (*apostolos*) has a similar meaning: a messenger or a "sent one." It seems undeniable that every single known being in existence—God, angels, and humans—all send (and are sometimes sent by) others from one place, in order to do certain jobs or tasks in other locations.

Allow me to dispense with the obvious—but unmistakable—truth this shows us. In order for Jesus to have been sent to us from the Father, he needed to exist somewhere apart from us in the first place. The same is true for the Holy Spirit. The same is also true for the angels, and for us. You cannot "send" someone to another place if they are *already there*. While I will not harp on this point, since I believe it has been made clear, this reasoning also applies to the "return" language that Jesus constantly used.

Throughout his ministry, Jesus reminded his followers that he would not be able to stay with them forever; at the right time, he would return to the Father (Jn. 14:28, 16:10). In fact, one thing Jesus said illustrated both the idea of being sent and the idea of returning in one powerful verse: "I came forth from the Father and have come

---

[62] See Luke 4:18 and 43, 9:48, 10:16, John 3:17, 5:36, 6:57 and 1 John 4:9-10 for just a few examples of this language.

[63] Refer to 1 Peter 1:12, John 14:16 and 16:7, for more examples.

into the world; I am leaving the world again and going to the Father" (Jn. 16:28). The account of Stephen's martyrdom speaks to this issue as well. When he had delivered his powerful message—which also sealed his fate—he saw something that must have provided him tremendous comfort in his greatest time of need:

> "But being full of the Holy Spirit, he gazed intently into heaven and saw the glory of God, and Jesus standing at the right hand of God; and he said, 'Behold, I see the heavens opened up and the Son of Man standing at the right hand of God' " (Acts 7:55-56).

There is much that could be unpacked here. For one thing, this is yet another example where the Bible describes heaven as a realm (the "heavens opened up"). But at present, the most important thing is that Stephen saw the "Son of Man"—which was an OT concept that Jesus applied to himself—"standing at the right hand of God." Further, he also saw the "glory of God" (recall Moses in Exodus 33). Clearly, God (the Father) was seen in a specific location, at a specific time, with the resurrected Jesus (the Son) by His side. What we know from Scripture is this: the Son was with the Father, then came into our world, then returned to the Father, and both were seen together *at a specific location* afterwards. What else is there to say? Well, maybe that one day he will *return* again to our world (Rev. 22:12). The future coming clearly suggests that Jesus is not currently on earth; he is somewhere else! But where? He is in heaven, with the rest of the heavenly beings.

Not only does all this show that God does indeed have spatial location (i.e. He is not everywhere at once), it also tells us something about time. As far as the biblical authors understood things, God exists in time. Recall Craig and Helm's sentiments above, where both admit that, while the Bible places God in time, many religious thinkers disagree. Here and now, I am not going to attempt to unpack Einstein's theory of relativity, the A and B theories of time, what static or dynamic views of time entail, or anything else connected to those weighty topics. There are plenty of places to read about these issues,[64] but they are simply beyond the scope of this book. Then again, we do not need to go so far in order to prove that God exists in time.

The primary reason we know this goes back to Jesus' statement in John 16:28 (and elsewhere); there was a point in time when the Son of God was not on earth with us, a point in time when he was, then yet another point when he returned to the Father in heaven. In other words, there was a "before" and an "after" in each of these cases. We all understand what that means. If you have children, you will particularly understand this point. There was a time in your life when your children did not exist, and then a time when they did. Perhaps nothing is more life-changing than that specific "before and after." In these instances, time is clearly what is at stake. The same is true about God in relation to any creative act, like the creation of the universe, animal life, or even human beings. All God's redemptive acts would apply as well: the calling of Abraham, the institution of both the old and new covenants, and the sending of His Son to bear the sins of the world. Every one of these things implies that something new had occurred, and that *times* had changed. The terms "before" and "after" clearly connote the existence of time, and God Himself has had many of both.

So, what is really the basis for believing that God exists outside of time? If the Bible, as a whole, depicts Him as existing in time—which most scholars readily admit—why would any Bible-believer reject this idea? There are several reasons why this is the case, and they primarily deal with how the deep issues of physics and cosmology factor into our perception of reality. As I previously mentioned, these issues go beyond the scope of this book and would take us way too far into the weeds. When it comes down to it, the

---

[64] For more on this issue, I refer you to Craig's *Time and Eternity* and Beilby's (editor) *Divine Foreknowledge*.

view that God exists outside of time primarily comes down to one thing: the belief that the universe came into existence from nothing, and that time itself began when the material world was created. The thought is that God existed in a timeless state prior to Creation, because there was no matter: no "space-time" reality. This assumes that the heavenly realm was created when our universe was, and that the "In the beginning" part of Genesis 1:1 is talking about the origin of every last part of reality: the heavens, the earth, all created beings (like angels), and anything else that might exist. To put it mildly, this view is not the slightest bit settled within the field of biblical studies, and a very strong case can be made that the heavenly realm existed before our own. Of course, there is also the matter that a universe from "nothing"—or even the existence of nothing in principle—has always been hotly contested and seems to be a logical impossibility to many (myself included). The age-old axiom that "from nothing, nothing comes" is about as logical a thought as one could ever hope to find.

I need to mention something else though. The truth is that the science involved in these matters is typically packed full of assumptions, and changes frequently. More than that, it is incredibly complex and difficult to understand. This is why I find it particularly curious that people are willing to use matters like special relativity or universal expansion to dual with the plain reading of Scripture. Why assume that the biblical authors were ignorant about God, or that God had revealed false information about Himself to them, in order to thread the needle of balancing Scripture with mainstream scientific views that are constantly shifting? This simply seems like a recipe for disaster and, in my experience, it usually is.

Besides this, the other major reason why it is often believed that God exists outside of time is the view that God knows the future. In order for God to know the future, He must not be bound by time as we are. Essentially, time would not apply to God. Here again, discussing this matter thoroughly would take us far from the main issues of this book. However, there are some quick problems worth mentioning. It is true that there are certain passages that could potentially lead us to believe that God knows the future. This is especially true for those who view many of the apocalyptic sections of the Bible—like Isaiah 24-27, Daniel 11-12, Matthew 24, and most of Revelation, to name a few—as being literal descriptions of events that will take place at the end of our world. A large portion of these types of passages are either clearly figurative or are very general in nature, while others would not involve God peering distantly into the future. A lot of these "predictions" about the future entail God telling us what *He is going to accomplish* at some point. If God vows to do something—like judge the world, destroy Satan, raise the dead, etc.— then we can have certainty that it will happen. In this sense, aspects of the future could be known to God because He knows He will fulfill His promises: not because time is not real or that the "future" has already occurred to God. With this being said, I do understand that this is a complex topic, and that there can be reasonable cases made for accepting that certain biblical passages reveal divine knowledge about events that are yet to occur.

However, there also passages to the contrary. As the Bible explains things, God is often emotionally distraught by the choices we make. Prior to the Great Flood, God became sorrowful that He created humanity (Gen. 6:6). God continuously pleaded with the Israelites (and sometimes other groups), promising them not to do what He was planning to do, if they repented (Jer. 18:8, Jon. 3, Zech. 1:3). If you think about it, this type of "*if* you do this, I will do that" negotiation occurs all throughout the Bible. As I will momentarily explain, none of these examples makes logical sense if the future is truly set, determined, and known by God in advance. Clearly, there are passages that can be used to make opposing cases about whether God knows the future. If, for the moment, we consider these passages to be a wash—determining that either explanation is possible, depending upon your view of Scripture—we must ask which would make the best sense overall. Ponder this, for example. If God does indeed know every single thing that will ever happen for the rest of eternity, then He must also know every single thing *that He will do* for the rest of eternity. This is absolutely inescapable. If God knows what He will do infinitely into the future (and always has known), then He cannot help but act according to what is set to happen. In other words, God's actions are just as fixed and determined as our own. In a sense, He is trapped: stuck doing what He knows He is going to do. If God were able to do other than what He knows He will do, it would mean that He never knew the future to begin with! I realize this may seem like a strange concept to most of us, but upon close inspection, it is difficult to avoid.

Also consider what this would mean about an issue like prayer. When we pray to God, we do so with the expectation that God can (and hopefully will) intervene to change the current or future outcome of something. God might provide healing, empowerment, comfort, or a myriad of other things. The thought, of course, is that our prayers can cause God to do what would not otherwise have been done. This is the definition of intercessory prayer: asking God to enact change in the lives of others is the obvious purpose. The Bible demonstrates numerous examples where people prayed to God for something, and He altered what "would have been" because of it.[65] But if you really think about it, this type of prayer would be utterly futile and pointless if the future is already set and determined. Why would we even think to ask God to change the outcome of future events if they have already occurred to Him? Why ask for God to

---

[65] Consider the following passages as examples: Ex. 32:11-14, Jon. 3:10, and Amos 7:1-6. God also attempts to negotiate with Abraham and was willing to toss aside his destructive plans for Sodom (Gen. 18:16-33). The problem was that Sodom did not turn out to have citizens worth saving!

intercede to cure someone of an illness, or to help us get a job, or even just to provide comfort, if these requests could not change what would ultimately happen? What can be done with this problem? It ends up looking something like this: we pray for "X" to happen (as God knew we would), then God responds to our prayer for "X" to happen (as God knew He would), then what God knew would happen with "X" to begin with indeed happens! Now, we may think we had some effect in all of this, but we didn't. Not really. You cannot alter what is inevitable, and what is already real to God.

In this short assessment, it may already feel like we have drifted away from the central point of the chapter. You may be wondering what this has to do with God and the angels having tangible form (i.e. bodies). Essentially, all of these things go together. Things that occupy space and exist in time also have some type of physicality or tangible qualities. There are items that exist which do not possess any of these characteristics. These items would be called "abstract objects." Abstract objects are very real, but they are not physical in nature. Examples of things that qualify as abstract objects would be items like numbers, thoughts, ideas, and information. All these things exist, but none can be physically encountered. Moreover, abstract objects have no spatial location. Where is the thought that the sky is blue? Where is the number eight? Yes, of course abstract objects are the products of, and apply only to, physical things. Thoughts and ideas are the products of brains. Numbers correspond only to the physical world. You get the idea. Of course, God is not a number or an idea; God is a conscious, creative, thoughtful, and most important, *living* being.

Not only are abstract objects immaterial realities, they do not exist in time, either. Sure, they *correspond* with physical things in real time, but they do not exist apart from them. Would the number nineteen exist if there were no physical world, and no intelligent beings to understand it? I would not want to be tasked with making the case that it would! Besides abstract objects—which, again, relate only to the physical world—no item or entity is truly immaterial; that is, not occupying any space. Abstract objects exist neither in time nor in space, and they are not physical in nature. On the other hand, all other things do exist in time and space, and are therefore tangible realities. I have attempted this, but I implore you to do the same. Besides numbers, ideas, thoughts, and information, name one thing that has no tangible qualities. Did you come up with any? I am betting not.

Fortunately, the Bible makes sense and corresponds with the world we inhabit. With regards to the issues I have discussed in this section, the biblical description matches the reality we know and understand. God, the angels, and all of humanity exist in time and space. The Son was "sent" by the Father to enter our world as one of us and, when his mission had been accomplished, he "returned" to heaven. The Spirit of God also "comes" and "goes" between our world and the heavenly realm, as indicated by all the language in the Bible. Even those who do not believe that God exists in time and space admit that the biblical authors did! Despite the fact that the Bible describes God as having spatial location, embodiment, and that He exists in time, most of us have been told the opposite. The same could be said about the angelic beings, and heaven itself. Hopefully, this trend is becoming obvious as the book progresses. This should cause us to stop and contemplate the possible motives involved in these efforts. Why is there such insistence on undermining the biblical message and pushing theological perspectives that obviously run counter to Scripture? I will now briefly address this important issue, because it has a great deal to do with virtually every part of this book and Christian doctrine in general.

The Rise of Immaterialism

Over the course of time, I—and others whom I know—have been accused of being a "materialist" because of the theological beliefs I hold. Merriam-Webster defines the intended type of materialism as follows:

> "A theory that physical matter is the only or fundamental reality and that all being and processes and phenomena can be explained as manifestations or results of matter."[66]

In other words, *everything* is reducible to physical causes and material phenomena. When one charges another with being a materialist, they basically mean that the person has no room in his or her worldview for something like a soul or a spirit, as well as anything that is immaterial or "spiritual." It is thought that materialists reject normative understandings of these topics, and so they are effectively either atheists or theists who live on "the fringe:" believers who dwell on the outskirts of what is considered to be solid religious orthodoxy. In a sense, this charge is valid; rejecting the typical views on these matters does put one on the fringe, so to speak. On the other hand, the Bible itself should probably be considered as a fringe text, since it describes the spirit, the soul, and spiritual things in ways that are *not* normative by today's standards. There is what the Bible says, and then there is what the average believer has been taught. Sadly, the two do not always align, and it is increasingly the case that they do not. Based on the previous sections of this book, I hope that reality is becoming clear.

With all the talk about materialism, and the incessant charge that those who do not identify with particular views of reality are "materialists," I have to wonder about those who cast the aspersion: especially those who charge other God-fearers with it. People of this brood are not the dreaded "M word" themselves, but can they be described—or perhaps

---

[66] Meriam-Webster, "Materialism."

labeled—with an appropriate term all their own? I believe so. If rejecting that God, the risen Jesus, the angels, the heavenly world, and even human beings after death, are all completely immaterial and non-physical makes one a "materialist," then perhaps the opposite is true. Maybe accepting that these beings and locations are immaterial and non-physical makes one an "immaterialist." If the materialist is obsessed with ensuring that everything is reducible to physical causes, then the immaterialist must be equally determined to make sure that everything is reducible to non-physical causes, right? At the very least, the immaterialist does not outright reject the existence of material things—as we live in a material world, and we are material girls (and guys)—but certainly looks upon them with disdain. As Plato—whom I would argue may have had a greater influence on modern Christian thought than the biblical writers themselves—detailed in his theory of Forms, the material world is but an image that points to the greater, immaterial realities.

This view has very deep roots in certain Greek philosophies, and perhaps equally deep roots within the church. This was evident even in the earliest churches on record. In Corinth, the church had come to accept a form of Gnosticism that caused them to virtually abandon concern for their physical bodies and what they did with them. There are many forms of Gnosticism, but one of the central unifying factors was a disdain for the material world and the elevation of immaterial qualities (like the inner spirit).[67] As one might imagine, when this view meets morality, there are disastrous consequences. The church at Corinth became quite perverse. There was, in the words of the apostle Paul, "immorality of such a kind as does not exist even among the Gentiles" (1 Cor. 5:1)! Having sexual relations with one's in-laws was perhaps on the extreme end of things, but moral depravity was so ubiquitous in Corinth that a name was created to describe it. The Greek term *korinthiazesthai* meant "to

---

[67] G.L Borchert, "Gnosticism," in the *Evangelical Dictionary of Biblical Theology,* 485-488.

live like a Corinthian."[68] The church had fallen right in line with the rest of the culture: an all-too-common occurrence, no doubt.

The problem is, such behavior is the logical end to any view that subjugates the material world to the "spiritual" world. If the body is inferior to the spirit and will someday be obsolete anyway, what difference would it make what we do with it now? The Corinthians were following certain Gnostic and Platonic teachings to their logical ends: completely to the letter. Not that it ever left, but many people in the church have just as negative a view of the material world as anyone in Corinth ever did. This disdain may not manifest itself in the types of moral debauchery that existed at that time and place (though for some, it probably has), but it does remain visible in multiple ways. The first is tied directly to what has been discussed in this book thus far: the rejection of what is plainly recorded in the Bible. At times, it is not merely a rejection of biblical teachings, but a complete reversal of them. What Scripture plainly reveals often cannot be accepted by its most respected interpreters. The text must be morphed, changed, and distorted to fit an "immaterialist" agenda.

To illustrate this point, consider a very clear example. One of the most startling displays of this mentality comes from the topic of Jesus' resurrection body. When asked about how believers presently should understand this phenomenon, Christian philosopher, William Lane Craig, had this to say:

> "So how should we conceive of Christ's resurrection body today? Christ in his exalted state still has a human nature; he did not 'enter back into God's own existence.' But Christ has exited this four-dimensional space-time continuum. Therefore, perhaps we might say that his human nature does not now manifest itself corporeally. Compare a tuning fork which is plucked and begins to hum. If the vibrating fork is placed in a vacuum jar, though it continues to vibrate, it does not manifest itself by a humming noise because there is no

---

[68] William Barclay, "The Letters to the Corinthians," 2-3.

medium to carry its vibrations. Similarly, Christ's human nature, no longer immersed in spacetime, does not manifest itself as a body. But someday Christ will return and re-enter our four-dimensional space-time continuum, and then his body will become manifest."[69]

How does Craig know all this? Spacetime, four-dimensional space-time continuum, "God's own existence," etc.: this does not compute. Comparing the Son of God to a device used to tune a musical instrument was probably a bad analogy, regardless of how you look at it. I can (almost) imagine our Lord, as he reverberates across the cosmos . . .. In any event, the intent cannot be missed: even though Jesus appeared time and time again with his resurrection body, it was somewhat of an illusion. He wasn't actually taking that body back to the heavenly world with him, as all the biblical references suggest. Rather, it merely looks like he has a body whenever he appears to us. Bodies—like all other tangible realities—are properties only of *our* world; God has no need for such things, particularly in the long term. That must be why He decided to make our material world to begin with, right?

This type of thinking goes right along with several things that have already been discussed. The "Jesus Diet" illustrates an area where the biblical descriptions—how the eye-witnesses, or those who were writing on behalf of the eye-witnesses, understood things—are not just rejected, but are turned completely on their heads. There are several examples of where angels physically appeared, and then ate a meal, with human beings. Abraham stood near angels while they ate (Gen. 18:8), and Lot later dined with them as well (Gen. 19:3). We also know that the risen Jesus—with his resurrection, or "spiritual body"—enjoyed food with his disciples (Lk. 24:40-43).[70] As Paul explained, Jesus' body was like that of the other heavenly beings: the angels (1 Cor. 15:35-49).

---

[69] William Lane Craig, "Jesus' Body."

[70] Elsewhere, John recorded that one hundred and fifty-three "large fish" were caught (and some eaten) at an appearance of Jesus (21:11). While they no doubt

Even though we are led to believe that real eating took place, the spiritual cognoscenti—the wisest and most learned of teachers—know better. The biblical authors did not understand what they were seeing, and a select few of us who are hundreds (or even thousands) of years removed from the events are now "in the know." These happenings were only cheap attractions; you buy your ticket and take your seat, but what you see is most definitely not what you get. It only *seemed* as though they were able to sit down to a meal with mortals. Since heavenly beings cannot possibly have bodies, nor digestive organs, they also could not possibly have eaten anything even if they had wanted to. This is exactly the opposite conclusion that Abraham, Lot, Peter, John, James, and authors like Luke reached. Who to trust, who *to* trust?

In my estimation, this reversal of the biblical accounts is more evident in how we see ourselves than anything else. How we view matters like our own nature and the afterlife reveals our immaterialist tendencies even more than do our views of the heavenly beings. Most within the church believe that death brings about the separation of a conscious spirit from a body that has been rendered useless. When we die, the immaterial "you" goes off to live with other immaterial beings, in an immaterial ether world we call "heaven." We have all heard statements like, "I know that Harold is looking down at us right now," or "Kathy is in a much better place." Naturally, this implies that the individual has left this tangible world and is now living in a place that is quite the opposite. More critical, however, is the outright disdain that exists for our physical bodies. Since I will address this issue directly in chapter four, I will spend no more time on it now. It is important to note that the church's overall belief in disembodied spirits is not a biblical view, and it speaks directly to the immaterialist agenda.

Earlier in this chapter, while discussing the corporeality of God, I broached a deeper subject that is at the root of this problem. To be sure,

---

gave many away, this was truly a feast!

Platonic thought is usually the central factor whenever immaterial qualities are placed above material ones. However, the desire to be intellectually superior to those around us—to be the "spiritual cognoscenti" of the world—is a problem particularly relevant here as well. Throughout Jewish and Christian history, and up to the present day, there has always been a group who deem themselves to be the *eruditi* of their day and age: the "educated" ones. Alternatively, the majority of God-fearing folk have been asked to don the apparel of the *simpliciores*: the "simple" ones. At the end of the day, it all comes down to this: to the *eruditi*, reading the Bible in any sort of straightforward way is unacceptable. Instead, we must pass its words through the filters of modern and ancient philosophy, contemporary sciences—like cosmology, physics, and even evolutionary biology—"advanced" hermeneutical practice, and frankly, false piety, in order to get down to the truth. Despite the calls for *sola scriptura* (only the Bible) and the declaration that anyone can find salvation within its pages, God worked with human authors to craft a text that requires its readers to possess expertise in almost every major field of inquiry. We cannot take the archaic authors of Scripture at their words. This is what the *eruditi* have always told the rest of us. Whether it came from the mouths of the more corrupt Pharisees, certain Church Fathers, or a fair percentage of Christian philosophers throughout history, this basic message has been vigorously preached to every generation of people. Trust me: you have been more influenced by this reality than you probably realize.

If you really think about it, immaterialism provides the ideal vehicle for such an enterprise. It allows the spiritual cognoscenti to reject every single aspect of our existence at face value, because the "truth" exists beyond the grasp of the average person. This "truth" can be neatly tucked away through the rejection of the world as we experience it and concealed behind an artificial wall of gaudy philosophical and scientific speculation. Put succinctly, immaterialism allows its wielders to tell the world that things simply aren't what they seem to be. Up is not up. Down is not down. Bodies are not bodies. The angels looked to have physical form, but looks can be deceiving; Jesus appeared to have eaten, but actually didn't; God seemed to have physically showed Himself to Moses, but it only *seemed* that way; so on and so forth. Therein lies the trick. If things are not as we—or the biblical authors, for example—see or experience them, then we must have help in understanding reality. Enter the immaterialists. Sitting high upon their fortress of intellectual superiority, they are eager to light a beacon for those walking the dark path of ignorance.

If this assessment seems overly biting, I assure you that it is supposed to. This is not simply a matter of craving power, but of perverting reality and a biblical worldview. Most immaterialists—those who bow to an immaterial "spirit world" of sorts, that is ultimately superior to the material world we find ourselves living in—are the product of the spiritual cognoscenti I have been referring to. These self-proclaimed intellectuals tell them what to believe, how to believe, and when to believe it all. If their interpretation is counter to the biblical explanation, that is of no consequence. In fact, the proper interpretation *needs* to be opposite of what we read in the Bible. "Proper interpretation" is what keeps the spiritual cognoscenti in business. Unembodied heavenly beings, disembodied human beings, fake angelic appearances, fraudulent feats of physicality, and all the like, are part of the "unreal world" that has been concocted by the spiritual cognoscenti and adopted by the immaterialists sitting in the pew next to us. Perhaps more often, they are standing in the pulpit ahead of us. This is the world created by the *eruditi* and accepted by the *simpliciores*. The goal of immaterialism is nothing short of the complete annihilation of what God has revealed through history and Scripture. The agenda is to place God out of time, out of space, out of body, and out of our comprehension. In the starkest of contrasts, the purpose of Christ is to bring God and humanity together in all those ways.

Chapter Three

Between Two Realms

For whatever reason, one of the storylines that stands out to me from my youth was the one depicted within the film, *City of Angels*. Though I cannot be sure, I think the biggest reason I remember this movie is because of its hit song, "Iris," by the Goo Goo Dolls. To this day, I find that to be an incredible ballad. That being said, the movie itself follows a very intriguing storyline. The first of the two main characters of the film is named Maggie, who was played by actress Meg Ryan. The second lead character was named Seth, and he was portrayed by actor Nicholas Cage. Seth—who is actually an angel—invisibly haunts the Los Angeles world of heart surgeon Maggie and those around her. As time goes on, both Maggie and Seth become enamored with one another, despite not *really* being able to interact. Maggie can feel the angel's presence, occasionally hear him, and even more rarely, actually see him. Seth, on the other hand, is able to track Maggie's every move with an almost divine power.

There is a beautiful and fascinating interplay that takes place between the two characters. Seth unassumingly observes Maggie at the hospital while she cares for her patients, at the library while she does some evening reading, and as she performs her day to day routines. Occasionally, he gives some small indication of his presence. As time goes by, he becomes enthralled with this creature of lower stature, and physically makes himself known to her. Finally, Seth does the unthinkable. Knowing that an angel cannot entertain an intimate relationship with a human being (according to the movie), he decides to step down and become one. Thus, he gives up heaven for a place on earth. The most interesting aspect of this is how it all occurs. Seth passes in and out of his unseen realm and into our world in a way that Maggie can only vaguely understand, but understand it she does. When Seth is present in our world, he is as real as you or me. When he decides to leave, he simply steps into heaven: an unseen world that somehow exists in, around, and over top of our own, and mostly without our knowledge. This is truly a powerful concept.

Elements of this scenario should sound eerily familiar to us. We have human beings and angelic beings who are both able to understand one another, each in their own way. They do not live in the same realm, and the human figure (Maggie) has far less of an ability to perceive the being of higher power (Seth) than he does. The thing that unites them is their points of contact: the little moments when their lives intersect. "Iris" may have piqued my interest as a child, but the film's interpretation of the way in which the heavenly realm relates to ours is definitely what holds my interest as an adult. In this chapter, I wish to explore the great many ways that God and the angels have chosen to interact (and still do) with us. Further, I want to suggest that occasionally, we are able to do the unimaginable: peer into their world.

Points of Contact

At present, we exist both within this world and the larger universe. The Bible strongly suggests that God and the angelic host exist in the heavenly realm—which I have discussed throughout the book, particularly in chapter one—and that they can interact within ours at will. Further, the Bible displays that one day we will all share in a new creation, where we will even have new bodies. I will spend significant time discussing these concepts in chapter four. It seems, then, that we are presently living between two realms. Through the heavenly beings, we are connected to their realm, even though we live in our own. At the same time, we get a glimpse of what life will be like at Christ's return.

One of the most mysterious aspects of life between the realms is the relationship we have with the angels. This ranges from seeing angels as a source of strength or comfort, to things of an extremely unusual nature, and all things in between. Throughout the biblical narrative, God often chose to reach out to people through His chosen messengers—the angels. Human beings were approached by angels all throughout the Bible. The angel Gabriel appeared to both Mary and Elizabeth, to discuss the coming of Jesus and his cousin John (Lk. 1:5-38). Angels appeared at the empty tomb and at Jesus' ascension, to help his followers make sense of things (Lk. 24:4). Angels appeared to many people throughout the Old Testament as well. By my personal count, there are at least twenty-one *unique* events in the Bible where angels physically appeared to individuals.[71] This does not count the numerous other examples that might qualify but could also be visions of some sort. Though I discussed this issue at length in chapter one, it simply must be mentioned that in *every* one of these instances—and some of which involved many angels appearing at once—the angels were embodied beings. They showed up in tangible form. According to the Bible, angels are not immaterial; they have bodies. This cannot be ignored.

More than simply acknowledging this fact, it is actually necessary that we adopt this way of thinking. The main reason is that the bodily nature of the angels helps to explain some of the odd ways that we are connected to them. Let's begin with one of the strangest

---

[71] See the following passages: Gen. 16:7, 19:1-29, 32:1-6, 32:24-32 (Hos. 12:4 as well); Nu. 22:22-35, Jdg. 2:1-4, 6:11-22, 13:3-21; 2 Sam. 24:16-17; 1 Ki. 19:5-7; 1 Chr. 21:15-30; Dan. 3:25; Mt. 4:11, 28:1-7; Lk. 1:11-20, 1:26-38, 2:8-15, 22:43; Acts 5:19-20, 12:6-11, 27:23; Rev. 1:1, 22:8.

issues within in the Bible: the Nephilim. The Nephilim were the giant people that existed in the ancient world. Their existence is not a matter of folklore or speculation: not in the Bible, at least. They are also referenced in the works of other ancient cultures, to be sure.[72] But if you trust in the teachings of Scripture, the giants really existed. Everyone who believes in the story of David and Goliath would have to accept this reality. Goliath, the great Philistine warrior, is said to have been "six cubits and a span" (1 Sam. 17:4). That is, he was about 9 feet 9 inches tall. Prior to taking the land of Canaan, the Israelites sent spies to scout the land. They returned with a shocking report about its inhabitants: "There also we saw the Nephilim (the sons of Anak are part of the Nephilim); and we became like grasshoppers in our own sight, and so we were in their sight" (Num. 13:33). The frightened spies revealed that there was not just one giant individual in Canaan, but many groups of them.

Speaking of the "sons of Anak," the Bible tells us that the Canaanites, Ammonites, and Rephaites (or Rephaim) were also associated with giants, or the descendants of the Nephilim. Further, we hear of a king named "Og." Og had descended from the Rephaim, and it is noted that his bedstead was about 13.5 feet in length and 6 feet wide (Dt. 3:11). Both his enormous bedstead and his connection to the Rephaim strongly suggest that he too was a giant person. To compound the evidence for the Nephilim, the Bible records that God had typically instructed His people to offer some concession of peace to the groups they were supposed to overthrow (Dt. 20:10-15). Curiously, this practice did not seem to apply to any of the groups related to the Nephilim. Instead, Israel was commanded to eradicate them: ". . . you shall not leave alive anything that breathes. But you shall utterly destroy them . . ." (Dt. 20:16-17). It appears that God

---

[72] For a couple quick examples, see the images found on the Abydos King List and the Victory Stele of Naram-Sin.

had a specific problem with the Nephilim, and that they were not simply comprised of your average ancient citizens.

This hostility leads us into what is probably the most intriguing issue concerning the Nephilim, which is their origin. They were the product of the "sons of God" and human women. If you have not looked very far into this issue, you are probably wondering who the sons of God are. In order to answer that question, it might be useful to begin with something that, on the surface, would appear to be entirely unrelated. However, I assure you that what follows is incredibly pertinent information. Without question, one of the most obscure statements the apostle Paul ever made to a church is found in the first letter to the Corinthians. While instructing the women there to wear their hair long—which was almost certainly in part to separate them from the pagan temple prostitutes, who often shaved their heads (1 Cor. 11:5)—Paul offered a rather peculiar reason for doing so: "Therefore the woman ought to have a symbol of authority on her head, because of the angels" (1 Cor. 11:10).

At first blush, this seems like an incredibly odd and out of place statement. Women should have a "symbol of authority" (long hair, in this case) on their heads, *because of the angels?* What possible connection could this matter have to the angelic beings? Unfortunately, Paul says nothing else about it, so it is nearly impossible to be absolutely sure what he meant. As Peter once noted, Paul was known to say things that simply flew over everyone else's heads: "His letters contain some things that are hard to understand, which ignorant and unstable people distort, as they do the other Scriptures, to their own destruction" (2 Pet. 3:16). This could very well be one of those places. However, we can make plausible suggestions about what he may have intended. In this situation, context is everything. Furthermore, we must also be aware of the historical realities that may have shaped Paul's thinking on the matter. We need to begin with the latter, and work our way up to what was occurring in Corinth.

Just prior to the Great Flood, an extraordinary event occurred. In fact, this event unquestionably had a part to play in God's decision to flood the earth to begin with. Genesis 6:4 says, "The Nephilim were on the earth in those days, and also afterward, when the sons of God came in to the daughters of men, and they bore children to them. Those were the mighty men who were of old, men of renown." The connection between this statement and what immediately follows hardly seems coincidental. As soon as these irregular beings appeared on the scene—thanks to the sons of God, mind you—God pledged to flood the earth. The very next thing Genesis records after introducing the Nephilim reads as follows:

> "Then the LORD saw that the wickedness of man was great on the earth, and that every intent of the thoughts of his heart was only evil continually. The LORD was sorry that He had made man on the earth, and He was grieved in His heart. The LORD said, 'I will blot out man whom I have created from the face of the land, from man to animals to creeping things and to birds of the sky; for I am sorry that I have made them'" (6:5-7).

Clearly, this is an issue that has dire importance to us in several respects. Now, don't misunderstand me; the people of that day and age do not get off the hook. While the sons of God and the Nephilim certainly had a part to play in God's decision to send the Flood, the corruption that existed within the human race was a major contributing factor. Believe it or not, this actually takes us several millennia into the future, to the city of Corinth and the corrupt church that called it home. When we factor in Genesis 6:2, the events leading up to the Flood might have significant bearing on Paul's instructions to the women there: ". . . the sons of God saw that the daughters of men were beautiful; and they took wives for themselves, whomever they chose." That's right: these strange beings were physically attracted to the women of the time. However, the text seems to imply that the feeling may not have been mutual. It leaves us with the impression that this group of entities sort of surveyed their options and took what they wanted, *period*. Of course, that is just reasonable speculation. Whatever the case, this passage certainly tells us some very important things.

Some scholars have tried to persuade us that the sons of God were actually mere mortals—no doubt because of the problems posed by alternative explanations—but there shouldn't be any debate on the matter at this point. The truth is that the "sons of God" (*bə·nê hā·'ĕ·lō·hîm*) were heavenly beings: angels. We can be certain of this for two major reasons. The first is that every single time this phrase was used in an ancient Semitic language, it concerned the angelic beings. It simply was not a term that was associated with the human race. The second reason is based on something we previously established: the Nephilim were said to be giant people, and the sons of God were said to have given rise to them. There is no reasonable way to account for the emergence of the Nephilim, unless there was something more going on than standard human procreation. Together, these two points make it almost undeniable that the sons of God were not only non-human entities, but were from among the angels.

This information adds credence to the belief that angels have bodies. It would be laughable to suggest that the sons of God found women to be attractive, took them as mates, and then bore children with them, even though they were incorporeal. This view would be completely opposed to the biblical information on these matters. That aside, this may also help us to understand the strange connection between the women in Corinth's hair length and the angels. It seems reasonable that at least certain angels found (or find) women to be physically appealing, and that Paul's instructions to the Corinthians came from a concern that such a thing could possibly happen to them too. While none of us can be certain that Paul had this notion in mind, it is probably the most likely explanation going.

Surprisingly, there may be another reason to accept this view. Consider, for a moment, the context of both situations. Genesis 6 describes a world that was so corrupt—so morally decadent—that God literally becomes grieved and "regrets" that He had ever made humanity (6:5-7). The same thing happens in 1 Samuel 15:11, when God laments having made Saul the King of Israel. As you would expect, many thinkers are eager to tell us that this never *really* happened, either.[73] God couldn't have genuinely mourned or regretted His decision, because that would suggest that He didn't know what would happen (thus, denying His complete foreknowledge)! Instead, this was just a way for God to relate to us through Scripture. As such, it does not describe how God actually felt. This is another strong example of denying what the Bible directly tells us, in favor of some lofty explanation that has no biblical precedent. This further reflects my premise that scholars tend to subvert the plain reading of the Bible in favor of a perceived "higher level" truth, but let's get back to the main issue. As Genesis reveals, "Then the Lord saw that the wickedness of man was great on the earth, and that every intent of the thoughts of his heart was only evil continually" (6:5). Because of this, as well as the existence of the Nephilim, God decided it was necessary to wipe the slate clean with a massive deluge.

When we evaluate the situation in Corinth, we see much the same type of activity. Previously, I mentioned that the moral depravity within that city was so pronounced that a pejorative term was created for it; *korinthiazesthai* meant "to live like a Corinthian."[74] More germane, the surrounding culture was so corrupt that it led to unthinkable evils within the church itself. Paul's letters to the Corinthians basically read like a giant parental lecture. Paul was clear that the Corinthians were extremely immature in their faith, and that they were only able to take "milk" rather than solid "food" (1 Cor. 3:2-3). The church was full of jealousy and strife (3:3). It was very divided by class, with the poor often being neglected (1 Cor. 11:22). They made a sacrilege out of the Lord's Supper, even using it

---

[73] Reformed theologian, John Piper, provides an excellent example of this thinking on his video, "Why Does God Regret and Repent in the Bible?"
[74] William Barclay, "The Letters to the Corinthians," 2-3.

as an excuse to get drunk (11:21-22). Naturally, they were also sexually perverse. Nowhere is this more evident than in Paul's comment in 5:1: "It is actually reported that there is immorality among you, and immorality of such a kind as does not exist even among the Gentiles, that someone has his father's wife." This example truly displays the depths of immorality that members of the church had sunk to. It seems as though the church was finding ways to surpass the cultural norms around them, which were already thought to be deplorable by many of the surrounding groups of the day.

It is obvious that both the moral condition of those destroyed by the Flood and the people of Corinth several millennia later left a lot to be desired. Who are we kidding—these were cesspools of disobedience. But what is the point? How does this connect to the sons of God and Paul's statement about the angels? It seems that there is a clear link here between the cultures at play and the arrival of the sons of God. Could it be possible that the sons of God showed up prior to the Flood because human beings had essentially invited them? Perhaps the extremely decadent lifestyles displayed by the pre-Flood peoples left them particularly vulnerable to the fallen angels, whom are attracted to such behavior. It stands to reason that Paul may have seen just that sort of shameful lawlessness within the culture (and the church) at Corinth, and that he had instructed the women to take certain steps to prevent the angels from forcing themselves upon them, as they had done before the Flood.

Based on the many tribes associated with the Nephilim, this appears to have been a practice that occurred without regard to a group's ethnicity or geographical location. If Peter—and many other biblical writers—was correct in saying that the devil "prowls around like a roaring lion, seeking someone to devour" (1 Pet. 5:8), it is not a stretch to believe that the most morally deviant places might draw special attention. Most who believe in Satan and the demons—whom are fallen angels, and evil "sons of God"—probably also believe that immoral behavior can bring about further temptation and more attention from unwanted guests. Biblically speaking, both the pre-Flood world and 1st century Corinth were a notch above most other civilizations in this capacity. It might be fair to say that these people were practically begging for unholy intervention.

If nothing else, these issues show us that it is indeed possible for certain angelic beings to feel attraction towards human beings and to actually act upon that attraction. We should all find this to be incredibly bizarre, but it is nearly irrefutable from a biblical perspective. Like UFOs, demonic possession, and other matters, Scripture affirms that the Nephilim were real and that they came about through the union of angelic beings and women. Attempts to explain away these occurrences or turn them into something more mundane are typically even less rational, and are most definitely contrary to the plain reading of Scripture. Believe it or not, the issue of the sons of God joining themselves with human women leads to another odd place. If angels (of the fallen variety, if nothing else) can be attracted to us, can we also find them physically appealing?

There is indeed a biblical precedent for this, and we have already discussed these events for different reasons. After the Flood and Tower of Babel debacles, our world did not cease to be corrupt. Unfortunately, it never has and never will. Another human annihilation event was necessary in two specific cities: Sodom and Gomorrah. Much like the pre-Flood world and the people of Corinth, the people of these cities were morally depraved. Similar to Corinth in particular, Sodom is even recognized with its own pejorative term (sodomy). We use this expression today, do we not? Prior to the destruction of these cities and others on the plain (Gen. 19:24-25), two heavenly visitors came to Lot. Their mission was of the common variety for angels: to deliver a message about something that was about to happen. In this case, they were there to tell Lot and his family to leave town before the entire thing was destroyed. Ultimately, everyone except for Lot's wife—who perished terribly in the event (19:26)—obeyed their instructions and were saved. An equally interesting thing happened before these events though. Apparently, someone in Sodom saw the two angels enter the picture, and the city's entire collection of male inhabitants became extremely interested. The reason for their curiosity could not be any more bizarre:

> "Before they had gone to bed, all the men from every part of the city of Sodom—both young and old—surrounded the house. They called to Lot, 'Where are the men who came to you tonight? Bring them out to us so that we can have sex with them' " (Gen. 19:4-5).

The men of Sodom were not there to welcome Lot's angelic visitors or to ask for a miracle; they were there to rape them.

As if this event was not weird enough, Lot's solution to the problem seems almost incomprehensible; he offers up his daughters instead (19:6-8). While no one should condone this action, Lot probably suggested it because there were strict rules regarding the hospitality of guests in those days, and he may have deemed it to be a better alternative than disgracing God's heavenly servants. In any event, it was hardly a noble proposition. Fortunately for Lot's daughters, the men of Sodom wanted no part of his offer. Instead, they tried to force their way into the house, in an effort to seize both Lot and the angels (19:9).

For the present purposes, the crucial aspect of this story is that the men of Sodom were utterly infatuated with these angelic visitors, and in an extremely sexual way. The text is emphatic that "... *all* the men from *every part* of the city of Sodom—*both young and old*—surrounded the house."[75] There was something appealing about these angels; they possessed an allure that no mortal man ever could have. At the same time, the angels were described as being "men" by Lot, the narrator, and the men of Sodom.[76] The oddity that angels were also referred to as men was common throughout the Old Testament, as I discussed in chapter one.[77] We can learn at least two important things from this: 1) The men of

---

[75] Gen. 19:4. Emphasis, mine.

[76] See 19:5, 8 and 10.

[77] Refer back to the section, "Lower than the Angels" for more on this connection.

Sodom were physically (and perhaps, supernaturally) attracted to the angels and 2) The angels strongly resembled human beings. They looked very similar to us, but clearly surpassed our appearance in some respect. This bolsters my overarching view that we are more closely connected to the angels than most of us can imagine, though we are not identical.

Though it probably doesn't need to be stated, these findings lead to a very uncomfortable issue. If the men of Sodom were physically attracted to angels, and the sons of God (fallen angels) were attracted to women, does this mean that these types of relationships will exist after the resurrection? Given the previous sections, this is a rather loaded question. This is increasingly the case when we consider other related issues. One would be—as many are quick to point out—Jesus' statement in Mark 12:25 (or Mt. 22:30). There, Jesus responds to an ill-conceived question from the Sadducees. In an effort to trip him up, they inquire as to who a woman would be married to after the resurrection, if she had been widowed by seven different men (brothers, in this case). Jesus' response was direct:

> ". . . Is this not the reason you are mistaken, that you do not
> understand the Scriptures or the power of God? For when they
> rise from the dead, they neither marry nor are given in marriage,
> but are like angels in heaven."

Beyond the obvious point that we will be "like the angels" after the resurrection, we are left to wonder what all that entails. I have repeatedly noted the biblical view that this involves physical embodiment. Additionally, Jesus reveals that marriage—the covenant between man and wife—will no longer exist as a function of society from that point on. However, does that suggest that *all* manner of physical relationships will cease to exist at that time? While both testaments of the Bible affirm that sexual relationships are not lawful outside of marriage,[78] it is only reasonable to

---

[78] See Dt. 22:13-30 and Mt. 5:27-30, for example. More specifically, 1 Cor. 7:1-10 is very clear that having only one spouse is permissible and that sexual relationships

believe that such a rule is not binding once our entire mode of existence has changed. There would be no *mortal* men and women that can marry, so to speak, since we will have been changed into something more like the angelic form.

Now, I am not suggesting that sexual interactions will just continue in the same way, much less that we will be able to freely indulge in such things because marriage will be obsolete. Rather, I am suggesting that Jesus' statement in Mark 12:25 does not directly designate that all relationships and attraction cease once we have been resurrected. Our mode of existence—probably including our laws, and certainly much about our current human relationships—will change at that time. To say, however, that none of these things will remain in any way, shape, or form is a jump beyond what Scripture has revealed to us. Jesus was making two points to the Sadducees, who rejected the afterlife. The first is that there is indeed life after death (resurrection), and the second is that resurrection life will not operate exactly like our lives on earth. The Bible does not reveal more details on this matter, but there is a precedent in place—as described with the sons of God and the Nephilim, the story of the angels near Sodom, and Paul's command to the women at Corinth—that sexual attraction can potentially still play a role within the heavenly realm, and perhaps even in the world to come. We cannot say this for certain, but the door is undoubtedly open to this reality.

This brings up a final enigma: does gender exist in heaven, and will it exist after we are raised from the dead? The Bible does speak to this issue, but certainly not directly. Have you ever noticed that there are no angels presented in Scripture who have female names? There are obviously angels with male names (like Gabriel and Michael), but no female names are present. Some have suggested that the two winged-women of Zechariah 5:9 are actually angels, but the context of the passage suggests that the women serve an entirely symbolic role, as they do in many other

---

outside of marriage are not.

metaphorical parts of Scripture.[79] Putting this verse aside, there are no others that tell of female angels. In terms of making a positive case, this cannot be done from Scripture. Nevertheless, if they do exist, it would not be surprising to see only male angels coming as messengers. When we consider that both the prophets and the apostles were all men, it seems rational that female angels would not be used in this capacity. Perhaps they exist but serve different roles than the male angels, similar to how human men and women operate.

One other thought might potentially lend support to this view. If we believe that there is some continuity between who we are now and who we will be after the resurrection, it seems illogical to suggest that gender will have no part to play in this. Our genders inform a great deal of who we are and how we experience the world. To eliminate this influence would be to devalue our resurrection experience and impair the connection between this life and the next. Jesus was born a man, and he experienced life as a man. He died as a man and was raised as a heavenly man. After the Resurrection, Jesus continued to be known to his followers by his actions and personality (discussed more in chapter four). In other words, the experiences and characteristics he possessed prior to the Crucifixion remained intact after the Resurrection. While this not an airtight case that gender exists in heaven or in the world to come, it seems like a reasonable conclusion.

The alternative is to assert that there is no gender at all among the heavenly beings, and that any assignment of male names or traits to angels in the Bible are superficial displays intended to help ignorant mortals understand spiritual realities. If true, all of us will be changed into a sort of homogeneous collection of heavenly beings at the resurrection. As I have

---

[79] The *Pulpit Commentary* summarizes the options as follows: "These two women who now come in sight have been supposed to represent the Assyrians and Babylonians, who wore the agents in the deportation of Israel; or else are considered abettors of the woman in the ephah, who for a time save her from destruction."

suggested throughout the book, this is a view with an agenda to undermine physical realities and the connection between earthly beings and heavenly beings. One must flip the biblical evidence on its head, rejecting what is clearly taught for something that is not. These matters no doubt place us in uncomfortable territory. However, our response should not be to dismiss them all as temporary displays or illusions. These are mysteries, not tricks.

Ancient Eyes

At various points, I have discussed the ways that God and the angels revealed themselves to our spiritual ancestors. Moses met with God on a regular basis, speaking with him "as a man speaks to his friend" (Ex. 33:11). More than that, God showed Moses "His glory," as He literally displayed certain parts of His body to Moses (33:18-23). Strike that; God falsely displayed His metaphorical exterior to a man who clearly thought he was seeing the real McCoy. That is how these types of events are explained to us. Scripturally speaking, Moses' encounter with God certainly seemed to be real and historically accurate. As I have shown, the Bible describes many similar examples throughout its pages. The modern man or woman, however, "knows better."

This is a major problem. As a young man who was trained in good old-fashioned exegesis—meaning, the practice of "drawing out" what the biblical texts originally meant, and in their original contexts—I was taught to first ask myself one very important question: what did the events described in the Bible mean to the original authors? Put another way: how did the people who both saw and recorded these events interpret what they had seen? This may be the first rule of biblical studies, but it also appears to be the most dispensable one. We have forgotten the principle that flesh and blood human beings chronicled the things we read about within the Bible. They saw floods, parting seas, bread that fell from the sky, strange flying machines (discussed in the next section), many miraculous events, and even the heavenly beings themselves. They saw these amazing things as you or I would, and they wrote about what they saw in like manner. They were guided by God, but *they* recorded what had occurred.

What I am getting at is this: it is imperative that we take the biblical accounts seriously, and as they were intended. How did the biblical characters interpret their experiences when they encountered God or the angels? That is the question. The question is *not*, how does the 21ˢᵗ century person view these events with respect to the appropriate philosophical and scientific influences? When Moses observed God as He passed by him in Exodus 33, he believed that he was really seeing the Almighty. When people saw the angels, they really believed they were physically present. When the apostles watched Jesus eat fish after the Resurrection, they truly believed that he ate the fish. Lot undoubtedly thought the same thing, when he hosted the two heavenly visitors. We know all this because that is what we find in Scripture. They recorded the events as *they* understood them. Let's not overcomplicate this.

Further reason for taking the biblical accounts as they were recorded comes from an unlikely source: other ancient writings. Of course, it may be unfair to say "unlikely," because this is one of the first places we should check when evaluating the events contained within the Bible. In my opinion—which is largely based on how the encounters were documented—there is continuity between the Bible and many of the surrounding works from antiquity. The biblical authors were not the only ones to record heavenly visitors. Far from it. Though both Jews and Christians have traditionally viewed the Bible as the supreme source of information on such matters (which I agree with), we must also consider the accounts of others whom God may have spoken to. Do we really believe that God was not interested in the rest of humanity, or that He did not attempt to reach out to them? It would be impossible for God to "so love the world" if He restricted His dealings with human beings to a relatively small group of ancient Hebrews, wouldn't it? Personally, I don't believe that is the case. Concerning the issues within this book, the testimony of other groups from the ancient world are extremely relevant. When we see the world through their eyes, we find further reason to believe in the existence of the heavenly beings. Additionally, we may even come away with a more complete view of the "spiritual things" we have discussed thus far.

To me, one of the most remarkable things in all the world is the fact that every major ancient culture believed in the existence of more powerful beings. When I say "every" major ancient culture, I mean *every* major ancient culture. The Egyptians, Sumerians, Mayans, Aztecs, Assyrians, Babylonians, Persians, Chinese, and the Australian aboriginal people: all accepted that we are not alone in existence. While some portray it as popular today, atheism—the belief that no deity exists whatsoever—has never been an overly accepted worldview. I suspect this is because it goes against every common-sense piece of evidence we have about reality. Today, atheism represents a mere 2 percent of the world's population, and some even suspect that it will decrease in the future.[80] If you add agnostics—those who simply "do not know" if there is a deity, or do not believe we could know one way or the other—into the mix, the number moves up to around 7 percent of the world's adult population.[81] Easily more alarming is the growing list of people called "nones," particularly within the U.S. and Europe. Think of these individuals as those who have absolutely no religious affiliations, almost as though these matters are not even contemplated. This group can be viewed as "post-religious," giving little or no thought to spiritual things one way or another. The fact

---

[80] See Chapman's article, "Global Study: Atheists in Decline" for more on this issue.
[81] See Zuckerman's article, "How Many Atheists Are There?"

remains, however, that those who thoughtfully consider—but ultimately reject—the existence of a deity has remained very low across the centuries.

While it is true that atheism and agnosticism have been around since about the 8th century B.C.,[82] the outright denial of a creator (or creators) was particularly rare among ancient cultures. Moreover, the *overwhelming* majority of people believed in and worshipped their chosen god/s with great fervor. One of the things they were most adamant about is creation: how it all got here, so to speak. When we look at some of the most prominent creation accounts that exist outside of the Bible, it becomes evident that everyone was generally on the same page. This is true with regards to the central features—the overall message the accounts are projecting—anyway. I would go so far as to say that we can see a divine hand involved in the way that the ancients understood our existence. If we look to the East, we see several interesting creation stories that have many parallels. One of the most significant traditions involves "Pangu." Pangu is the name given to the creator of all things, and it is believed that he alone existed in a type of chaotic state where heaven and earth were mixed together.[83] Pangu allegedly slumbered in something resembling an egg and, after awakening to realize he is trapped, he cracked the shell and broke out. In doing so, Pangu split the egg and created the sky above and the earth below. This was how the heavens and the earth were separated and organized.

Another account comes from a religion that has noted similarities with Christianity and Judaism: Zoroastrianism. Dating to around the sixth century B.C., this account holds that Ahura Mazda—or, the one "wise Lord"—existed alone in Endless Light while his evil counterpart, Ahriman, lived in Absolute Darkness.[84] Here, you

---

[82] I refer you to Whitmarsh's book, *Battling the Gods: Atheism in the Ancient World*, for an in-depth discussion of atheism in the ancient world.
[83] E.C. Rammel, "Pangu and the Chinese Creation Story."

have a clear reference to a beginning of our realm and the separation of light and darkness. Perhaps more intriguing, the Zoroastrian creation account holds that Ahura Mazda progressed from making plant life, to animal life, and finally to fashioning human beings. One of the most ancient creation stories comes to us from Babylon. The *Enuma Elish*, which is recorded on tablets dating back to at least 1100 B.C., describes a primordial world like the one we read about in Genesis 1. The first of the "Seven Tablets" reveals the following:

> "When in the height heaven was not named, And the earth beneath did not yet bear a name, And the primeval Apsu, who begat them, And chaos, Tiamut, the mother of them both. Their waters were mingled together . . ."[85]

Heaven is placed above the earth, with water "mingled" around in a chaotic state. This is very much how the Hebrew creation narrative explains the origins of our universe.

Creation wasn't the only major event these groups agreed upon; they also held that divine beings were responsible for our annihilation. Specifically, the ancient cultures affirmed the biblical story of a massive flood that was used to wipe out humanity. Beyond the Bible, the most popular flood story comes from the Mesopotamian *Epic of Gilgamesh*. Among many other interesting things, it mentions that a "raging flood-wave" destroyed "walls of stone" and the sacred sanctuaries.[86] Interestingly, the account also reveals that a man named Utanapishtim was commanded to build a massive floating vessel to save himself and to preserve our race.[87] Concerning the Flood, one early Sumerian story discusses the union of incredible windstorms and a flood that swept over their cult centers.[88] Putting these accounts together with the

---

[84] Jacques Duchesne-Guillemin, "Zoroastrianism."
[85] *Enuma Elish: Epic of Creation*, Tablet 1.
[86] The Epic of Gilgamesh, Tablet I.
[87] Ibid. Tablets I and IX.
[88] See "Sumerian Myth."

biblical story of Noah and the Flood, we have ample reason to believe that such an event happened. However, other major civilizations—and even most of the smaller cultures on record—have a story verifying that this occurred. In truth, we have more than three hundred flood stories spanning the globe.[89]

As a final example, I must mention a very curious motif that spans the ancient world: the serpent. While this figure had relevance in many places, the people of Teotihuacan most notably displayed a deep adoration for what they called the "Feathered Serpent." This eerie creature—which was also popularly called Quetzalcoatl, by the Aztecs—grew to nothing short of god-like status to many people living near the pre-Columbian Americas (collectively referred to as the "Mesoamericans").[90] It was typically portrayed as a long, snake-like creature that possessed feathers (or wings) on various parts of its body. The feathers are quite prominent around its head, making it somewhat resemble a lion. It is almost universally accepted that the serpent aspect is supposed to display its relationship to the "earthly realm." It moves along the ground like all other worldly creatures.

However, the Feathered Serpent was not a being with earthly origins. For one thing, its feathers suggest that it had supernatural powers and that it could ascend to the greater realm of existence: the heavens. However, it was believed to have come from the world below. The Temple of the Feathered Serpent—which is thought to have been built near the end of the 2nd century B.C.—exhibits several rather mysterious qualities.[91] Beneath the pyramid is a collection of interconnected tunnels, all leading to a three-chamber core in the center. The people of Teotihuacan sprinkled powdered pyrite on the ceilings to create a "starry sky" appearance. On the ground were rigid carvings that mimic the earth's terrain, and sculptures of people gazing

---

[89] Christopher Snyder, "Did the Story of Noah Really Happen?"
[90] See the article, "Quetzalcoatl," at Encyclopedia.com.
[91] See "Mythical Beasts: Blood for the Snake God." S1E5.

at the stars above. The most peculiar feature of the lower area of the complex is that the chambers were intentionally flooded with liquid mercury, in an effort to produce a large underground lake. This was an *extremely* extensive process. It is believed that they went to these lengths in order to create a mini-cosmos in the depths of the ground: a miniature "underworld," so to speak.[92] The Feathered Serpent was supposed to have come from—and to have greatly preferred—this watery underworld, but was able to ascend or descend to reach all three great realms of existence: the underworld, the earth, and the heavens. In other words, it had a role in heaven, hell, and our world.

The most intriguing aspect of the serpent phenomenon is the spatial and temporal separation of the groups that either celebrated or disdained these icons. As a clear example, Teotihuacan—which was located at the modern-day Valley of Mexico—is nearly 8,000 miles away from Israel. Those who were deifying the Feathered Serpent lived on the opposite side of the world from the Jewish people of the day. Speaking of which, the serpent is a tremendous character in the Bible as well. A serpent deceived Adam and Eve, causing sin to enter the world (Gen. 3). That same serpent is later identified as a horrible and treacherous monster (Is. 27:1). As time went on, we came to understand that the serpent is Satan himself: a fallen angel who possesses incredible power (2 Cor. 4:4, Rev. 20:2). In addition to Israel and Teotihuacan, homage to great serpents was paid in Africa, Egypt, Asia, and North America. Not far from where I grew up, the Great Serpent Mound of Ohio is evidence of the latter. It was constructed by the Adena culture, or perhaps an earlier group of Native Americans, to house their dead. There can be no question that serpents were either worshipped as deities or condemned as devils all over the ancient world. It seems that such a phenomenon cannot be explained apart

---

[92] Ibid.

from beings of higher power, who revealed the significance of this figure to cultures around the world.

While so many other examples could be cited, these items demonstrate a crucial fact of history: almost all the ancient cultures on record experienced heavenly visitors. They often received very similar explanations about how the world was created, as well as the details concerning certain major events that occurred thereafter. This tells us that God did not limit His outreach efforts solely to Jews and Christians. God, the angels, and even the demons, have all profoundly influenced the entire world. Contact between us and the heavenly beings is an almost ubiquitous phenomenon across the globe and throughout history. While the Bible certainly holds primacy in the Christian life (or should, at least), "spiritual things" transcend us and are not restricted only to what we understand from Scripture. The types of activities and beings described by the biblical authors strongly resemble those often depicted by other groups of the ancient world. What Moses, Ezekiel, Paul, and so many others experienced is much like what many around the globe had. This is more reason to believe that we doubt their accounts—or attempt to subvert them—at our own peril. But perhaps nowhere is this correlation more obvious than in the way the heavenly visitors, and the location they ventured from, were described. We now turn to this very topic.

Sky Beings

The majority of ancient cultures believed that they were visited by, and were even created by, "sky beings." This view was so entrenched within their communities that they drew pictures of these visitors on rock structures and often created earthworks that are visible only from the sky. As researcher Erich Von Däniken has pointed out within his many writings, these scattered groups typically portrayed their heavenly visitors with luminous faces, brilliant auras around their heads, halos, and many other similar physical characteristics.[93] One very prevalent example is the native inhabitants of Australia, or the Aboriginal people. Almost every one of these dispersed tribes believed that they had been created by beings that hailed from beyond our world. Of particular interest was their fascination with *wondinas* (mother goddesses), who were often depicted with rays or halos around their heads. Across the globe in North America, the Hopi people inscribed oddly similar visitors onto rock, sometimes even doing so at heights of several meters.[94] Speaking of which, the legendary Nazca Lines in southern Peru are an incredible example of artwork that was clearly intended to be seen from the sky. That region is also full of rock drawings that would go right alongside of those created by the Aboriginals and the Hopi. In what is now northern Guatemala, the Mayan temple structure at Tikal directly corresponds with the Pleiades constellation. That area of space is where the "sky beings" who made them were thought to have descended from. I have addressed this topic in much more detail elsewhere,[95] but these examples illustrate that the people of the ancient world appeared to have been obsessed with visitors from "above."

Just like the biblical characters, these ancient groups were really seeing these figures. As they understood things, the visitors were both incredibly real and tangible. The "sky beings" were an almost ubiquitous phenomenon in ancient times. Though it may come as a surprise to many of us, nowhere is this belief more apparent than in the Bible. A consistent theme running throughout its pages is that heaven is "up there" or "above" us, and that earth is "down

---

[93] Erich Von Däniken, *Evidence of the Gods*, 69-82.
[94] Ibid. 83.
[95] For those who are more interested in this topic, and how "extraterrestrials" fit within the biblical story in general, I refer you to my book *God Made the Aliens: Making Sense of Extraterrestrial Contact.*

here" and "below" the heavens. There are a couple major reasons for this. The first is that the very first verse of the Bible makes this clear: "In the beginning God created the heavens and the earth" (Gen. 1:1). As the Creation account unfolds, we discover that "the heavens" (*haš-šā-ma-yim*) of 1:1 are synonymous with the sky. In fact, every time this term is used in the rest of the account, it is referring to the sky above us.[96] Religious philosophers have developed an unfortunate habit of interpreting Genesis 1:1 as referring to the creation of *all* things (including the heavenly realm), even though it most naturally reads as pertaining only to our world and the sky above us. At best, it may be referring to the whole of our universe, but that would probably be stretching the text beyond its intention. This effort is of course a means to an end. Specifically, it helps to support the various cosmological arguments—generally positing that the formation of our universe (or even the whole of existence) requires a deity. Predictably, these usually end up being "immaterialist" in nature. Immaterial realities are superior to material ones, and must also be the root cause of them. It always seems to come down to these foundational views.

With this said, heaven is sometimes seen as a place in the sky because the language of the Creation narrative indicates it. Simply put, the heavens and the sky can function synonymously. The second reason is that the heavens—meaning here, God's abode or the "heavenly realm"—is also discussed as being "up there," above the earth. Consider the famous statement found in Isaiah 66:1: "Thus says the LORD, 'Heaven is My throne and the earth is My footstool. Where then is a house you could build for Me? And where is a place that I may rest'?" This is clearly intended to imply the image of God sitting in the sky, with His feet resting upon the earth. Jesus echoed this notion in his

---

[96] I refer you to Genesis 1:9, 14, 15, 17, and 20 for just a few examples. Genesis 1:14-18 clearly states that the sun and moon were placed in the *haš-šā-ma-yim*, which clearly tells us that we are dealing with the sky.

Sermon on the Mount: "But I say to you, make no oath at all, either by heaven, for it is the throne of God, or by the earth, for it is the footstool of His feet . . ." (Mt. 5:34-35). Here again, God's dwelling is in space, and his feet reach down to touch our world.

However, it should be obvious that these are metaphorical statements: *genuine* statements of allegory, as opposed to those often contrived to be taken that way. If God truly exists above our heads, and rests His feet here amongst us, we probably would have noticed. I may be going out on a limb there. But there are more literal ways that we see this idea show up in Scripture. In chapter two,[97] I mentioned that the Bible continuously uses the language of "coming," "going," and "returning" to describe Jesus and the other two members of the Godhead. This, among other things, only makes sense if all three persons have spatial location (which would further suggest some type of physicality). Along those lines, the Bible describes God as both ascending and descending; up to heaven and down to earth, as expected.

In truth, this language pervades many parts of both the Old and New Testaments. So, does this mean that heaven is indeed in the sky after all? Well, not exactly. There is a clear connection between the sky over our heads and the heavenly realm inhabited by God and the angels. If you think about it, do we not sometimes find ourselves peering into the sky when we pray, or when we are entranced in spiritual contemplation? I know I do. There is something very intuitive about it: something natural. When the apostle Paul spoke of his trip—whether that took place physically or in a vision, he could not say for certain—to the "third heaven," he also spoke of being "caught up" into it (2 Cor. 12:2-4). Paul used the exact same word (*harpazō*) in 1 Thessalonians 4:17, when he described Christ's return and how the living will be "caught up" to meet him in the air. At the

---

[97] Please refer back to the section, "Time and Space" for review.

same time, Paul spoke extensively about heaven as another realm of existence entirely.[98] The word used in those passages (*epouranios*) does not just mean "heavens" or the "sky," but something above or surpassing these concepts. It literally means "above" the heavens or the sky and refers to the heavenly sphere or the sphere of spiritual activities.[99] This is probably the same thinking behind Paul's "third heaven" or his reference to "paradise" (2 Cor. 12:4). In this, the connection between heaven and the sky is unmistakable.

If—as I have shown again and again—the heavenly beings can simply pass between the two realms of heaven and earth, why do they also go up to heaven and come down to earth? Notice that some of the most impactful parts of the biblical narrative display the concepts of ascending and descending. At Jesus' baptism, the Spirit descends upon him (Mt. 3:16). During the Ascension, when Jesus says goodbye to his followers once and for all, he rises into "the heavens" (the sky) *before* vanishing (Acts 1:9). At Christ's return, he is described as descending to earth (1 The. 4:16) with his army of angels (Mt. 25:31). Even the fall of Satan is described with similar terminology: "I was watching Satan fall from heaven like lightning" (Lk. 10:18).

These examples show us something very important: going up into the sky and coming down to earth are clearly the best ways we can imagine how the world of the divine connects to our own. If the Spirit simply appeared from nowhere at the Baptism, the event would be far less of an amazing spectacle. If Jesus had just vanished at the Ascension, the grandiose nature of his final exit would have been almost entirely lost; his followers would have been left asking, "what exactly just happened?" Can we even imagine Jesus' return (or any return) without visualizing him "coming back" to us? Finally, what could better illustrate Satan's punishment than a long and tumultuous

---

[98] See Ephesians 1:3, 20, 2:6, and 3:10
[99] Strong's Greek Concordance, 2032.

fall through the sky? "I was watching Satan as he instantly slipped into a new realm" doesn't quite hit the mark.

While God and the angels can indeed come into our realm and leave their own, they occasionally make a spectacle of their comings and goings. It makes sense that this may be done for illustrative purposes; it happens so that we might better understand. It's not that they aren't (at times) really ascending and descending, because they are. It's just that they do not *have* to come and go that way. I'll say this again, as it is worth repeating: the heavenly beings do not have to ascend and descend, but sometimes do in order to better illustrate something to us. These acts are for us, not for them. In this assessment, it has hopefully become obvious that the heavens and the sky can be synonymous expressions. However, heaven—as the realm of the angels and the abode of God—is not in outer space. All this talk about travelling to and from the sky does offer one more item to consider, and it is even further "out there" than anything discussed thus far in the chapter.

There are few issues in the world that invoke a wider range of opinions than unidentified flying objects. The very mention of UFOs—and the newer expression, UAPs (Unidentified Aerial Phenomena)—can make sane men into fools and fools into wise men. There is plenty of skepticism and unfettered excitement to go around, and probably in equal parts. Personally, I think the evidence for UFOs is overwhelming at this point. There are other beings out there, and they have flying crafts of a highly-advanced variety. This has become so apparent in recent years that even the U.S. government—which has long been among the least forthcoming institutions in the world on this matter—has announced the need for a more formal process of recording unexplained sightings. In 2019, spokespersons from the Navy issued the following remarks to Politico:

> "There have been a number of reports of unauthorized and/or unidentified aircraft entering various military-

controlled ranges and designated air space in recent years. For safety and security concerns, the Navy and the [U.S. Air Force] takes these reports very seriously and investigates each and every report. As part of this effort, the Navy is updating and formalizing the process by which reports of any such suspected incursions can be made to the cognizant authorities."[100]

As one might expect, this statement was not intended to imply that all these unidentified aircraft are celestial in nature. However, there is no question that some aircraft fit this category. This reality is undeniable when we consider that esteemed aeronautical experts, retired Air Force pilots, and many commercial airline personnel have reported sightings that could not have been attributed to anything we here possess.[101] Far from being a localized issue, eyewitnesses—and even video recordings—are virtually flooding in from all over the world. Regardless of the source, it is almost unanimously recognized that the majority of sightings are never even reported. For those who believe in the Bible, but doubt this point, it may come as a surprise to know that the sacred texts have something to say on the subject.

While the heavenly beings can either ascend or descend on their own, Scripture reveals that they sometimes do so in flying vehicles. As strange as it may sound, it seems as though the topic of UFOs takes us to another point of contact: a place where we live between the two great realms. When the angels appear in their spaceships (so to speak), we suddenly find ourselves somewhere between heaven and earth. For that fleeting period, the two realms intersect. There are several events recorded in the Bible where human witnesses found themselves in this

---

[100] See Bryan Bender's article in Politico, "U.S. Navy drafting new guidelines for reporting UFOs."
[101] I highly recommend Leslie Kean's, *UFOS: Generals, Pilots, and Government Officials Go on the Record*. Kean discusses a multitude of highly-respected sources who have gone on the record with their UFO encounters. The evidence presented is staggering.

mysterious and unfamiliar territory. Specifically, three events come to the forefront.

First, we have the most famous of the three: Ezekiel's infamous vision of heavenly beings. Realistically, the whole of Ezekiel 1 should be read, because the particularities of the prophet's personal encounter are scattered throughout the chapter. Overall, there are several critical points that should be considered. First, descriptions like the "flashing lights," "glowing metal in the midst of the fire," "spinning wheels," and the like, are difficult to interpret as anything other than flying vehicles. Second, the winged appearance of the four "living beings" is consistent with many other descriptions of the angels in Scripture. No matter how you look at, the wings are intended to signify flight. The heavenly vehicle and the beings who attended it (or perhaps, operated it?) are associated with air travel.

Second, we have the prophet Elijah and his ascension into heaven. 2 Kings 2:11-12 reads as follows:

> "As they were going along and talking, behold, there appeared a chariot of fire and horses of fire which separated the two of them. And Elijah went up by a whirlwind to heaven. Elisha saw it and cried out, 'My father, my father, the chariots of Israel and its horsemen!' And he saw Elijah no more."

The "chariot of fire" most definitely sounds familiar to the craft Ezekiel saw, and it unquestionably descended from the sky. Whether or not the whirlwind that carried him away was directly associated with the chariot is unclear, but it would not change the fact that the chariot had some role to play in the event. More than that, Elisha (Elijah's successor of sorts) immediately cries out—no doubt in astonishment—that he was seeing "the chariots of Israel and its horsemen." The angelic host is described on numerous occasions as travelling in these "chariots," terminology which I have suggested elsewhere should be considered as the ancient equivalent of the modern "vehicle." The angels quite clearly pilot sky or space vehicles.

I have saved the best example for last. Elisha and his personal helper—while being surrounded by an Aramean army—saw not one, not two, or even a small group of angels in their flying machines, but enough to cover an entire mountainside:

> "Now when the attendant of the man of God had risen early and gone out, behold, an army with horses and chariots was circling the city. And his servant said to him, 'Alas, my master! What shall we do?' So he answered, 'Do not fear, for those who are with us are more than those who are with them.' Then Elisha prayed and said, 'O Lord, I pray, open his eyes that he may see.' And the Lord opened the servant's eyes and he saw; and behold, the mountain was full of horses and chariots of fire all around Elisha. When they came down to him, Elisha prayed to the Lord and said, 'Strike this people with blindness, I pray.' So He struck them with blindness according to the word of Elisha" (2 Ki. 6:15-18).

I quoted part of this passage earlier in the book, but included a couple more verses this time. The reason why is that this text has significant meaning at the present, because it shows several things simultaneously.

First, it proves yet again that the angels indeed have flying crafts, and that there are hundreds (if not thousands) of them. Second, it describes the acts of ascending and descending; the chariots appear on the mountain tops but are clearly able to descend and come to Elisha's aid. Lastly, it shows that heaven—the abode of God and the angels—is *not* in the sky, but is a different realm altogether. We know this because the angels appear to Elisha and his servant out of nowhere; the angels were near to both of them, even though they were not previously visible. In this one passage, everything I have been suggesting about the existence of UFOs in the Bible, the reality of the heavenly realm, and the connection between heaven and the sky, is clearly visible. Here, the angels appear high up in the sky in their heavenly vehicles, and come from an unseen realm of existence. They show that they can appear in our world in an instant, but that they can also travel through space. This further clarifies how heaven can be both "up there" and somewhere outside of our universe entirely.

It seems that the heavenly beings are also sky beings. We understand them as having a very strong connection to the cosmos above us, and so did most of the ancient cultures on record. This helps to explain the phenomenon of UFO sightings, and why these crafts tend to simply vanish after they have been seen in the sky. Where do they go, if not into a different realm or dimension? Furthermore, this represents another means by which we know we are living between two realms. Like Elisha's servant, we spend most of our time in our own world, having little to no knowledge about what is occurring in heaven. But occasionally, we see that world appear before us. Heaven comes into our realm to meet us. Undoubtedly, the biblical characters saw the heavenly beings ascend, descend, and pass between the two great realms. We must now press on, because these are not the only ways we find ourselves living in the middle of something larger than ourselves.

(War) On Earth as it is in Heaven

It has been estimated that the total number of fatalities resulting from the wars of the 20th century may exceed 150 million people.[102] Sadly, this could be a conservative estimate. As wonderful as it is that we have not seen a World War in the 21st century, it is also a horrifying prospect. What are the chances that we won't see one (or more) in this century? Not good. With the destructive capabilities that many countries now possess, it

---

[102] See the Piero Scaruffi article, "Wars and Casualties of the 20th and 21st Centuries."

could well be that the next World War will be the last. Obviously, we all pray that such a thing does not happen. With that said, it is not just our realm that has seen the bitterness of combat. Oddly enough, it seems that the heavenly realm has also experienced this misfortune. Stranger still is the fact that we find ourselves caught in the middle of it. We are all squarely within an ongoing battle between the heavenly forces of good and evil.

Though it takes some piecing together, we can understand how it came to be that Satan and his multitude of angels fell from grace: there was war in heaven. It is nearly impossible to tell when this all occurred, and there is even debate as to when the angelic beings were created to begin with. I will not go into great detail on this, because it would take us a bit off course to do so. In short, the question revolves around how one views the Creation account in Genesis 1. Is the "In the beginning" part of verse one referring to the beginning of the universe, the beginning of *all* things that exist anywhere and everywhere (even the heavenly realm), or is it more of a symbolic statement about the start of our area of the cosmos and the human project in general? How we answer these questions can have significant bearing on many theological issues,[103] but that is for another time.

Concerning the angels, it also has a lot of importance. If the text is talking about the creation of our universe or simply the human story, then it is quite possible that the angels were created at some time prior to what Genesis 1:1 discusses. If it is talking about all things that exist *period*—our entire realm of existence, the heavenly realm, and perhaps things we may not even know of—then the angels may have been created at (or near to) the time that everything on earth was. I tend to believe that it is far too

---

[103] This would be true of things like the cosmological arguments for God's existence and whether Creation was done *ex nihilo* (out of nothing) or *ex materia* (out of existing materials), for a couple of examples. The basis of cosmological arguments is that the emergence of anything (like a universe) from nothing requires the existence of a god. You can see how cosmological arguments are tied to an *ex nihilo* view, and that both are heavily affected by how we interpret Genesis 1:1.

presumptuous to interpret Genesis 1:1 as referring to all things that exist anywhere and everywhere. For one thing, it feels extremely selective to take that verse so stringently literally, but to take parts of what immediately follows as being as being metaphorical (which virtually everyone does). At times, the first verse of the Creation story is about the only one interpreters take literally.

Setting that aside, we do not know exactly when the angels were created. Additionally, we do not really know when they fell from their heavenly existence, either. That may have been before the creation of our realm (a view I subscribe to), but it could also have been at a time after it was created. We do know, however, that the angelic fall—and of course the battle as well—took place prior to the fall of man. This is a certainty, since Satan (in the form of the serpent) was there to tempt Adam and Eve (Gen. 3), and so he must have fallen prior to that time. Though the timeline for these events is difficult to discern, we have much more clarity on what happened between God and the disobedient angels.

In truth, the role of Satan and the demons is nowhere near as prominent in the Old Testament as it is in the New Testament. Information is scant in the OT, but not completely absent. Satan shows up to cast accusations in Zechariah 3:1-3, and to both accuse and afflict Job (1:13-2:7). He is described as a serpentine monster (Leviathan) in Isaiah 27:1, and this creature shows up in various other passages.[104] Of course, Satan's first appearance is narrated in Genesis 3, when he helped guide Adam and Eve into disobedience. None of these talk about how or why Satan—and probably the other fallen angels—ended up as the chief opponent of God and His people, but they certainly illustrate that he had indeed become that. To get to the heart of these questions, we have to jump way forward in the Bible. In order to get to events that occurred even deeper in the past, we have to reference texts that were written even further into the future. You have to love the Bible!

---

[104] See Job 3:8 and 41:1, as well as Psalms 74:14 and 104:26.

The truth is, a great deal of information we have about both the past and future battles between the fallen angels and God's army comes from the book of Revelation. This is important to note, because Revelation is a highly metaphorical and enigmatic book in many respects. This does not mean it is false, it just means that the truths expressed are often not of the historical variety; they did not (or will not) *literally* happen. The same could be said of Jesus' many parables. In Revelation, look no further than the images of beasts coming out of the sea (13:1-10), or the arrival of the half man/half locust creatures we read about in 9:1-12, just to name a couple. However, there are things in Revelation that are clearly historical in nature and are intended to be taken literally. John's presence on the island of Patmos (1:9), his encounter with the Lord (1:10-18), and the existence of the seven churches (cc. 2-3), are obvious examples. With that said, the overwhelming amount of what we read in Revelation can be debated concerning whether it is literal or metaphorical. Both types of writing reveal truths, but they both do not reveal truths as they actually occur in reality.

This realization is important regarding all things in Scripture, especially the apocalyptic writings. The fall of the angels is no different. Within Revelation, we read several amazing things about this issue. The first thing is that Satan opposes humanity, especially God's people. In chapter 12, a "woman" gives birth to a "male child." The child is immediately threatened by a great "red dragon," who seeks to devour him. It is almost unanimously accepted by commentators that the woman symbolizes Israel, the child symbolizes Christ, and the red dragon symbolizes Satan. This makes sense; Israel gave rise to Christ (the Messiah), whose mission Satan wanted to destroy. It is what happens directly after this that is so mysterious though:

> "And there was war in heaven, Michael and his angels waging war with the dragon. The dragon and his angels waged war, and they were not strong enough, and there was no longer a place found for them in heaven. And the great

dragon was thrown down, the serpent of old who is called the devil and Satan, who deceives the whole world; he was thrown down to the earth, and his angels were thrown down with him" (12:7-9).

Here, a great battle in heaven is depicted. On the one side, we have the archangel Michael and other mighty angels. On the other, we have Satan and his crew of rebel angels. When the dust cleared, the latter group was hurled down to earth. This defeat did not stop them, however. We read later in the chapter that Satan set out to make war with the rest of God's children (12:17).

The age-old question about this passage has been, does it reflect something that *has* occurred, something that *will* occur, or even both? Does this symbolize the fallen angels' castigation from heaven in the distant past, or does it point to a time when that will happen? In the strange world of Revelation, it is possible that it points to both in one way or another. All of chapter 12 reads as incredibly symbolic, so is it a stretch to take the battle descriptions literally? Well, probably. It would certainly be very selective to do so, at the least. However, it may not matter in the slightest. As previously mentioned, metaphorical truth is still truth. Whether the events are to be taken literally or not, the passage still points to the reality that a separation exists between the good heavenly beings and the evil ones; Satan and his demons have become opponents of God and His holy angels.

In line with the idea that Satan was thrown down to earth is Jesus' statement in Luke 10:18, when the apostles were stunned that demons obeyed him: "And He said to them, 'I was watching Satan fall from heaven like lightning.' " There are some translations that go ahead and place this statement squarely into the past tense ("I watched"), but the NASB correctly translates this word (*etheōroun*) in the Greek "imperfect tense," which here reflects an ongoing action that occurred in the past. Jesus was carefully observing Satan's fall from grace, and that fall continues to have incredible significance today. This was not an event that simply occurred and the story ended. Rather, it occurred and continues to have bearing in our lives. This is especially true when we consider just how powerful Satan is said to be. Paul referred to him with descriptions like "the god of this age"[105] and the "prince of the power of the air" (Eph. 2:2). During Jesus' temptation, Satan reveals an interesting point that Jesus did not dispute: "I will give You all this domain and its glory; for it has been handed over to me, and I give it to whomever I wish" (Lk. 4:6). Satan has ruled this age (on earth), but make no mistake about who will rule the next: Christ. Let's not forget that many angels chose to follow Satan in his betrayal, as do scores of human beings. This reality is deeply troubling, but is true nonetheless. Satan is a very powerful entity.

Not only does it appear that the forces of darkness were cast out of heaven, it also seems as though they will be defeated in battle again in the future. Revelation of course mentions this event, saying:

> "When the thousand years are completed, Satan will be released from his prison, and will come out to deceive the nations which are in the four corners of the earth, Gog and Magog, to gather them together for the war; the number of them is like the sand of the seashore. And they came up on the broad plain of the earth and surrounded the camp of the saints and the beloved city, and fire came down from heaven and devoured them. And the devil who deceived them was thrown into the lake of fire and brimstone, where the beast and the false prophet are also; and they will be tormented day and night forever and ever" (Rev. 20:7-10).

John was shown a terrible vision: Satan and his forces will rally the troops one last time, in an effort to overthrow the Creator. As Revelation indicates, it will not go as planned. This is also revealed in 2 Thessalonians 2:8: "And then the lawless one will be revealed, whom the Lord Jesus will overthrow with the breath of his mouth and destroy by the splendor of

---

[105] 2 Cor. 4:4. Many translations interpret this text as "ruler" (of this age), but the Greek literally says "god" (*theos*).

his coming." The prophet Isaiah may even have alluded to this reality hundreds of years before Jesus walked the earth, when he said that God would one day destroy the great sea serpent called "Leviathan" (Is. 27:1). Even the demons freely admitted that there would be an "appointed time" when they would be destroyed (Mt. 8:29). This is clearly an allusion to Christ's return and the destruction of evil that will ensue.

This leads to another interesting aspect of this saga: we are caught in the middle of it all. The demons that admitted to their ultimate demise were making the most of their remaining time. In that particular case, they had possessed two men and were terrorizing the entire area through them (Mt. 8:28-34). Presently, the forces of evil behave much like rabid animals that were just loosed from their cages. 1 Peter 5:8 could not illustrate this point any more clearly: "Be of sober *spirit*, be on the alert. Your adversary, the devil, prowls around like a roaring lion, seeking someone to devour." Of course, we know it is not just Satan who looks to destroy lives. The New Testament is replete with examples of demons interfering in human activity. We have the two men previously mentioned, a man in a synagogue (Lk. 4:31-37), a young girl (Mk. 7:24-30), and even a demon who was literally attempting to murder a young boy by either burning or drowning him (Mk. 9:14-29). These are just a taste of the demonic carnage that exists in the Bible, and both Jesus and the apostles were well known for driving them away from helpless victims.

There are also less obvious ways that malevolent entities impact our world. Satan's successful overthrow of God's intentions with Adam and Eve have had everlasting effects. Though there is much debate about how intense the Fall was, and what its overall implications are, it is nearly impossible to doubt that it resulted in a less than preferable—and a less than intended—state of existence. All human beings suffer from what I like to call FBS; that is, "Fallen Body Syndrome." This is obvious to the young and old alike. All of us break bones, get the flu, suffer from various ailments, and sometimes develop debilitating or even lethal diseases. Who among us can watch a St. Jude's commercial, or any of the like, and not be emotionally stirred? One of the saddest and most frightening realities in the world is that children can suffer and die the same as anyone else.

I also think of other striking examples, like Joseph Merrick (the "Elephant Man") and Jonny Kennedy ("The Boy Whose Skin Fell Off"). After many years and false diagnoses, it was discovered that Merrick suffered from Proteus syndrome. This extremely rare disease is known to cause lesions on lymph nodes, overgrowth of one side of the body, an abnormally large head, and partial gigantism of the feet. Merrick displayed these symptoms in abundance, as can be seen in pictures all over the internet.[106] After being probed, ridiculed, and just plain tormented, Merrick died (no doubt painfully) at the young age of 27. Kennedy also suffered from a very rare condition called dystrophic epidermolysis bullosa (DEB). DEB typically causes the skin to blister, and sometimes leads to skin cancer. Needless to say, it can be *extremely* painful. Jonny's skin would peel off when his clothing or bandages were removed, resulting in a pain that few of us can imagine. He was born with no skin on his left leg, and died of a terrible form of skin cancer at the age of thirty-six. Both Merrick and Kennedy serve as powerful reminders to us all, but display only a taste of the possible afflictions we can face. In so many respects, ours is a fallen realm.

Deadly ailments are not the only struggles to contend with. Almost every other aspect of human existence displays our fallen nature. The roles that suicide, homicide, mental illness, sexual infidelity, and pornography play in the world are utterly devastating. According to the Centers for Disease Control and Prevention (the CDC), suicide rates in the U.S. have steadily risen since the turn of the twenty-first century. From 2000 to 2016, the age-adjusted suicide rate increased about 30 percent. This moved the number of suicides from about 10.4 per 100,000 people to 13.5 over that span, and this number has been on the increase since 2016.[107] The issue of people taking the lives of others has always been a

---

[106] Mary Kugler, "The Joseph Merrick Story."
[107] See the CDC article, "Suicide Rates in the United States Continue to Increase."

serious problem. As previously mentioned, most estimates suggest that more than 150 million people died in the 20th century by either the direct or indirect results of war.[108] Many believe that the more appropriate number might even surpass 200 million.[109] This of course says nothing about the global homicide rate, as well as rapes and assaults, which are all nearly impossible to reasonably estimate.

Looking at issues of sexual infidelity, is estimated that as many as 60 percent of married persons will participate in an act of unfaithfulness at some point during their marriage, and that nearly half of all marriages will end in divorce.[110] This says nothing about relationships outside of marriage, which are even more problematic much of the time. A major factor now involved in these issues—thanks mostly to the internet—is pornography, which has become so ubiquitous that researchers can hardly estimate its consumption. Some international studies have placed male usage between 50 and 99 percent (yes, 99 percent), and female usage between 30 and 86 percent.[111] In truth, the real numbers are probably closer to the higher figures, since many who are polled deny their involvement to save themselves the embarrassment. Sadly, there are a plethora of other issues that could be discussed. Humanity is a sick piece of brokenness. FBS is simply an everyday part of life, to one degree or another.

In essence, this is the war against "the flesh" that is spoken of throughout Scripture. Unlike the battle against the physical flesh that was previously discussed, this battle takes place within each of us; it is the battle of carnality, depravity, and temptation. It is extremely important to remember that Satan and the demons have a significant role in our mess. The world can be incredibly harsh, and the rebellious angels are at least part of why it is so. All this shows the ominous predicament we find ourselves in. In some sense, we are collateral damage: beings harmed by a

---

[108] See "Wars and Casualties of the 20th and 21st Centuries," for data on this issue.
[109] See "Estimated Totals for the Entire 20th Century."
[110] See "Facts and Statistics About Infidelity." This was based on U.S. findings.
[111] See Kirsten Weir's article, "Is Pornography Addictive?"

war that we neither asked for nor can completely comprehend. In another sense, we are involved in this battle every day. None of us are innocent, for we have all invited—in some way, and at some time—this war into our lives. Willful participation in sinful behavior, attempts to contact non-living or non-human entities, and even the basic failure to spiritually prepare ourselves against evil, are examples of things that give demonic forces a solid foothold. But we do not fight alone, thankfully. The unseen world of heavenly beings fights alongside us; God fights alongside of us. Moreover, we are actually called to battle: to *spiritual* warfare. The apostle Paul made this clear in his letter to the church at Ephesus:

> "Finally, be strong in the Lord and in the strength of His might. Put on the full armor of God, so that you will be able to stand firm against the schemes of the devil. For our struggle is not against flesh and blood, but against the rulers, against the powers, against the world forces of this darkness, against the spiritual *forces* of wickedness in the heavenly *places*. Therefore, take up the full armor of God, so that you will be able to resist in the evil day, and having done everything, to stand firm. Stand firm therefore, having girded your loins with truth, and having put on the breastplate of righteousness, and having shod your feet with the preparation of the gospel of peace; in addition to all, taking up the shield of faith with which you will be able to extinguish all the flaming arrows of the evil one. And take the helmet of salvation, and the sword of the Spirit, which is the word of God" (Eph. 6:10-17).

Make no mistake about it, this is war.

While we know how the story ends—and so do the demons, by their own admission—it does not change the fact that we are all involved in the cosmic battle of good and evil. This battle is going on all around us, both within our world and in the unseen heavenly realm. It is certainly perplexing to wonder how these beings can continue their campaign against God, even when they know of their certain destruction. But this is the nature of evil. Evil beings do not necessarily need to prevail, because that is not their *chief* mission. Rather, their top priority is to cause as much destruction as possible: to take as many people down with them as possible. Do we not know many people in this world that have the same agenda? Winning is great, but is more a fortunate byproduct of the chaos, and it is the chaos that matters most. Our part in this brings to mind something that Aragorn said to the reluctant King Theoden in *The Lord of the Rings: The Two Towers*: "Open war is upon you, whether you would risk it or not." Open war is upon all of us, whether we would risk it or not. Those who do not feel like any of this is going on around them, or that they do not even perceive such a thing to exist, are still involved. Chances are, they have unknowingly committed to a side already. If the darkness has left you alone, it may be because you are closer to it than you realize; those who pose no threat tend to get little attention. Satan needs pawns as badly as he needs queens or bishops. If the heavenly beings in no way relate to you, then it may be that you have closed yourself off to them. Both scenarios speak to the same result. Though we cannot avoid the battle, we can certainly choose who we will fight for. This is the most serious and consequential choice that any of us will ever make.

With all the talk of Satan, demons, and the spiritual war that rages on, there is one more item that needs to be discussed. Throughout this book, I have described that there are two major realms of existence: heaven and earth. If this point has been missed, please feel free to either delete the book from your chosen device or use the paperback as a fire starter. With that said, it is now apparent that there is actually a third realm of existence described within the Bible: the realm of hell. The reason I have not discussed hell alongside of heaven and earth is that it is truly the outlier of the three. It is not the outlier because the concept isn't equally interesting, or that it is not a very serious matter. Hell is the outlier because it doesn't exist. Well, it doesn't exist for anyone *yet*, I should say. Jesus spoke very frequently about hell, or what he called "Gehenna." Gehenna is the final and ultimate place of destruction for Satan, the demons, and unrepentant human beings (Rev. 20:10, 15). Hell is their *eventual* fate, not their present one.

This belief should be beyond dispute. Jesus stated this very clearly while speaking about the judgment of the wicked: "Depart from Me, accursed ones, into the eternal fire which has been prepared for the devil and his angels" (Mt. 25:41). The word translated here as "has been prepared" is *hētoimasmenon*, and is what we call the "perfect tense" in biblical Greek. This is used when something has been accomplished in the past but reaches to the present in terms of its implications. The NASB hit this nail on the head: hell has already been created (or is ordained to be created) but is not yet occupied. I have discussed this in greater depth elsewhere,[112] but the essential point is that no one is currently living in hell: not Satan, not the demons, and certainly not deceased human beings. Hell will undoubtedly be an extremely unpleasant reality for those unfortunate enough—but are nonetheless deemed to be deserving—to be sentenced there. It's just that it is not their reality at the present time.

When we put all the pieces of this section together, we see that war exists in more ways than we may ever have conceived. Human beings war against each other. Angels war against angels. Humans and angels are locked in battle. Combat took place before we ever existed. It still takes place now, and it will take place in the future. More important than our enemies, however, are our allies. Both God and his holy angels fight alongside of us and, as the Bible so famously declares, "If God *is* for us, who *is* against us?" (Rom. 8:31). This is yet another place where God and all His created beings are united; we are all involved in this, with some on the side of good and others on the side of evil. "Spiritual things" play out in our world every day in myriad ways, like our relationships, our physical health, our mental well-being, and, ultimately, our everlasting fates. These are not abstract ideas or vapid feelings; these are the realities that drive our physical world.

---

[112] See *The Death Myth*, pp. 78-84, for more about why hell is a future existence, not a present reality.

Joining Voices

While the previous section divulged some rather sobering realities about how our realm connects to the heavenly realm, we must also remember that there is beauty to be found in this relationship too. It's not all about war. On the opposite side of the spectrum, there is the excitement of gatherings where scores of created beings worship their Creator. Like the matters discussed in the previous section, worship transcends our world and serves as another place where the two great realms—and the beings who occupy them—overlap and unite. As we will see, there is worship on earth, in heaven, and even a type of worship that goes beyond anything we ever thought existed. We will begin with a quick word about the worship we best know and understand.

While alarming, it probably comes as no surprise to most of us that church attendance in the U.S. is on the decline. It has been for some time now, especially among young people. Various polling groups have reported that church attendance has hovered around 40 percent of the population for the last several decades, but there is reason to believe it is nowhere near this high. Along with others who have investigated this, a 2005 study in *The Journal for the Scientific Study of Religion* concluded that the actual number of people who are regularly attending church services is more like 17.7 percent.[113] How can we explain the disparity between 40 percent and 17.7 percent? The explanation may be what is called the "halo effect." This is the term used when people attempt to report things that tend to be viewed as more positive, like estimating a low number of sexual partners or downplaying past drug use. In this case, the number of people who were *reporting* that they attend church was far less than the number

---

[113] See the *Church Leaders* article, "What's the latest on church attendance in America," for more on this.

who were *actually* attending.[114] Polls that were based on head counts of attendees have exposed those that rely on verbal response.

"Across the pond," the news is even more discouraging. As of 2017, studies showed that participation in the Church of England (the C of E) hit a record low of 14 percent.[115] Worse, the number of young adults involved in the C of E fell to around 2 percent of the population. As most of us understand, churches are now predominantly comprised of those who are near to, or have surpassed, retirement age. It has long been known that keeping young people in the church is a major issue. I should also mention that church buildings are not the only places where worship is performed, but these statistics are symptomatic of our time. If these problems are combined with the rise of the "nones" (discussed previously),[116] then we have an even more serious predicament to contend with. Now, it is also true that both the Christian faith and church attendance are growing in parts of the world—especially in areas of Africa, India, and South America—and we should certainly rejoice in this fact. At the same time, the trend of diminished religious belief and communal worship in the West is extremely disheartening. It seems that worship on earth is a mixed bag, and it always has been. Overall, we clearly fail to exert the appropriate levels of praise and adoration that God deserves.

However, it can easily escape our attention that we are not the only beings in existence who pay homage to the Creator. Worship occurs within the heavenly realm, and it is performed by none other than the angels. Humanity may be lacking in this capacity, but I don't see God having quite the same issues in getting the angels to come and worship Him! This is probably especially true, since the angels live with God in the

---

[114] Ibid.

[115] See Sherwood's article, "Attendance at Church of England's Sunday services falls again."

[116] I talked about the "nones" in the last chapter, in the section "Ancient Eyes." "Nones" are those who simply have no religious affiliation whatsoever. Beyond even choosing whether to believe, religion essentially does not exist in their world in any way.

heavenly realm; they are not separated from His presence in the ways that we are. At various points in the Bible, we read about the worship that occurs in heaven. The book of Nehemiah records the following:

> "You alone are the LORD. You have made the heavens, The heaven of heavens with all their host, The earth and all that is on it, The seas and all that is in them. You give life to all of them And the heavenly host bows down before You" (9:6).

In reverence to God's amazing creative powers, all the beings of heaven bow before Him. Revelation reveals the same type of events: "And all the angels were standing around the throne and *around* the elders and the four living creatures; and they fell on their faces before the throne and worshiped God . . ." (Rev. 7:11). Later in the text, the angels cry "Hallelujah" at the destruction of Babylon—a symbolic name deriving from the ancient kingdom—and the reign of God (Rev. 19:3-6). Another clear example of angels worshipping God comes to us from the prophet Isaiah:

> "In the year of King Uzziah's death I saw the Lord sitting on a throne, lofty and exalted, with the train of His robe filling the temple. Seraphim stood above Him, each having six wings: with two he covered his face, and with two he covered his feet, and with two he flew. And one called out to another and said, "Holy, Holy, Holy, is the Lord of hosts, The whole earth is full of His glory" (6:1-3).

Besides this serving as another example where God is portrayed—both in visions and in literal appearances—in a tangible way, this displays a group of angelic beings singing praises aloud to God.

For our purposes, perhaps the most interesting aspect of heavenly worship is that it frequently overlaps with earthly events. This is the final type of worship I described in the introduction: the kind that "goes beyond anything we ever thought existed." There are numerous examples I could mention, but three really come to the forefront. The first involves what is unequivocally the greatest point of contact between heaven and earth in all of history: the birth of Christ. This was *the* event that showed God's solidarity with humanity, and the strong association between heaven and earth. While believers stand in awe, praising God each Advent season in jubilant expectation of Jesus' birth, the angels were actually the first beings to ever do so: "And suddenly there appeared with the angel a multitude of the heavenly host praising God and saying, 'Glory to God in the highest, And on earth peace among men with whom He is pleased' " (Lk. 2:13-14). The angels appeared from nowhere—as I have suggested they normally do—praising God for the entrance of His Son into our world. Not only did they praise the Father for sending the Son, they also praised the Son, who was found in human form: "And again, when God brings his firstborn into the world, he says, 'Let all God's angels worship him' " (Heb. 1:6). When they worshipped Jesus, they worshipped *both* God and man. This is an incredible thing to ponder!

While celebration deservedly broke out in heaven at the birth of Jesus, we also know from Scripture that it happens for us. That's right—for you and me. In Luke 15, Jesus tells a series of parables that speak to how valuable every human being is to God. From the Lost Sheep, to the Lost Coin, and finally to the Lost Son, Jesus described the significance of those living apart from God finally turning to Him. Of particular interest is the Parable of the Lost Coin, which reads as follows:

> "Or what woman, if she has ten silver coins and loses one coin, does not light a lamp and sweep the house and search carefully until she finds it? When she has found it, she calls together her friends and neighbors, saying, 'Rejoice with me, for I have found the coin which I had lost!' In the same way, I tell you, there is joy in the presence of the angels of God over one sinner who repents" (Lk. 15:8-10).

Just as the woman who found her silver coin rejoiced, the angels rejoice when one of us seeks God and turns away from the broken path. Though people certainly seek salvation in various ways and at different places, one popular method is to approach the altar during a church service. Typically, people will be gathered around to pray for the person giving his or her life to Christ and will later celebrate the event. But consider this: the angels also gather around these individuals and celebrate right alongside of us (in the heavenly realm) because of it! Though we do not always see it, this is another place where worship in heaven and on earth intersect.

Looking at the book of Hebrews, another major way that heavenly worship is connected to our own can be seen in 12:22-24:

> "But you have come to Mount Zion and to the city of the living God, the heavenly Jerusalem, and to myriads of angels, to the general assembly and church of the firstborn who are enrolled in heaven, and to God, the Judge of all, and to the spirits of the righteous made perfect, and to Jesus, the mediator of a new covenant, and to the sprinkled blood, which speaks better than the blood of Abel."

Nowhere in Scripture is our connection to God, the angels, and the heavenly realm more clearly and succinctly articulated. While some want to use this as proof that deceased believers currently live in heaven— "the spirits of the righteous made perfect"—it has nothing to do with that. In context, the author of Hebrews was comparing and contrasting the nature of the old and new covenants. Throughout the text, the covenant made through Moses is depicted as being completely inferior to the one instituted through Christ. Just prior to this passage, the old covenant is even described as an ominous reality. There is mention of a mountain of blazing fire, darkness, gloom, a whirlwind, and an overall sense of dread when the Israelites were at Mount Sinai (12:18-20). Even Moses said, "I am full of fear and trembling" (12:21)! By contrast, the new covenant was nothing of the sort. Unlike Mount Sinai, Mount Zion—which is used here as a spiritual counterpart to the earthly Jerusalem, and synonymous with the "heavenly Jerusalem"—represents a picture of hope and liberation.

This passage in Hebrews is about all the incredible realities involved in the new covenant. Jesus, not Moses, is the mediator, and the blood used to institute this covenant far surpassed the power and efficacy of any blood used throughout the Old Testament. Here, all who follow Christ and have been incorporated into God's Kingdom join with "myriads of angels," and even God Himself, in one existence. Whether it is the redeemed here on earth or the holy ones in heaven, we all share in this covenant. This is a place where the two realms of heaven and earth overlap; the veil is pierced, and we have spiritually joined the heavenly host. We do not physically see all this here and now, but it is true nonetheless. As difficult as it is to imagine, this reveals to us that we do not worship alone. Wherever and whenever we raise our voices in worship, there is a good chance that the angels are doing the same. More than that, this passage points forward to something else altogether. Though we are presently connected to those in heaven because of Christ's life, death, and resurrection, we also look to a time when we will literally and physically live with the heavenly beings not just with a new covenant, but within a new creation. Though Jesus drastically changed what it means for us to live between the realms, he also showed us that something greater awaits; there is a new world to come.

Chapter Four

The World to Come

It was the 2nd century Roman emperor (and stoic philosopher), Marcus Aurelius, who wrote: "Time is a sort of river of passing events, and strong is its current; no sooner is a thing brought to sight than it is swept by and another takes its place, and this too will be swept away." He also recorded that, "Everything that exists is in a manner the seed of that which will be." Though Aurelius authored many such sayings over the course of his life, these two truly resonate with one another. The first speaks to the fleeting nature of all things. Everything that comes to be in our world will someday cease to be. This applies to money, titles, relationships, and even our own lives. Further, these things are always replaced by something (or someone) else. As one thing becomes obsolete, another thing fills the void, and then the thing that filled void becomes obsolete and needs to be replaced. On and on the cycle goes. The author of Ecclesiastes (Qohelet) knew this as well as anyone who has ever lived, remarking that *everything* is essentially "breath."[117] As one breath comes, it soon passes, and another takes its place. As philosophers, rulers, and incredibly powerful men, Qohelet and Marcus Aurelius had quite a lot in common. It is no surprise they came to such similar conclusions about the nature of life. Like Qohelet, however, Aurelius did not use this pattern as a

---

[117] Traditionally believed to be King Solomon, Qohelet's name means the "assembler." In all his travels, luxuries, and experiences as king, he repeatedly concluded that everything was "vanity" (more literally, "breath" or "vapor"). None of these things truly last, and each experience simply gives way to the next. For further discussion about the author of Ecclesiastes and the meaning of the book, I highly recommend Crenshaw's, *An Introduction to the Old Testament* (247-250).

vehicle to depression or hopelessness. The second quote discloses that, even within this redundant series of events, there is purpose and meaning. Everything that happens in our world gives rise to other things. What happens now is connected to what happens next. In this, there is a natural flow and an order to our world.

Still, one cannot help but feel that the cycle must be broken: that it cannot go on forever. Put another way, all this cannot simply be a means to another means. Our world, our history, our lives, and everything that occurs therein, must ultimately be heading somewhere. At some point, there must be a resolution. Given the fallen nature of our world, this seems especially to be the case. Fortunately, the Bible does not describe reality as an endless cycle of events without a climax. To the contrary, it describes a pinnacle of history wherein our realm fully merges once more with the heavenly realm. In a sense, our world is the "seed" of that which will come, just as our bodies are seeds of the bodies that we will later receive at the resurrection (1 Cor. 15:35-38). Indeed, this entire story is heading for a decisive conclusion. What will occur thereafter cannot—and should not—be known to us at this time. In this chapter, we will discuss everything that we can hope to expect at the end of human history. Along the way, we will continue to see all the places where our lives intersect with God, the angels, and the world in which they inhabit. We begin by discussing the end of our personal stories, and by evaluating one of life's most vital questions: what happens when we die?

Heaven is Not Our Home

Sing the wondrous love of Jesus, sing his mercy and his grace; in the mansions bright and blessed he'll prepare us a place. When we all get to heaven, what a day of rejoicing that will be! When we all see Jesus, we'll sing and shout the victory.[118]

I recall an article I read years ago by the biblical scholar, N.T. Wright. The title of the article is the one I have adopted for this section of the book: *Heaven is Not Our Home.*[119] In it, Wright wisely flips traditional thinking almost entirely on its head. His overarching point in the article is simple but poignant: dying and going to heaven as a disembodied spirit is not the goal of the Christian faith. To the contrary, a *bodily* resurrection is the goal. On this point, Wright is entirely right. However, I would diverge with him on something very important. While Wright still sees us as living in disembodied form during the interim period—the time between death and the resurrection—I do not, nor do I believe that Scripture communicates this. If we could modify the title of the article just a bit, it would read perfectly; *Heaven is Not (Ever) Our Home.* It would come as a surprise to most people to learn that they are not heading for the "pearly gates" of heaven, and that E.E. Hewitt's classic hymn (above) is not entirely on target. We will not "all get to heaven."

This is not true simply of the unrepentant, but of the redeemed also. Not even the saintliest of deceased people can (or will) be found there. The belief that fallen believers will depart to heaven—as disembodied spirits, traditionally—at the moment of death is one of the most common beliefs within the church. In fact, it is difficult to imagine a view that has gained more popularity over the course of church history, especially the last couple centuries. The problem is, it is also difficult to find a belief that has been more contrived, less proven, and makes less sense of the biblical information than this one. In reality, the Bible does not teach that heaven is the goal of the Christian faith, or that it is even a stop along the way. More than that, it certainly doesn't tell us that we will go anywhere— *anywhere*—as disembodied spirits. Despite the emotional desire many of us have to adopt this belief, it does not naturally align with Scripture.

You are no doubt wondering why I would make such claims. Am I rejecting the afterlife? Don't I realize that life after death is one of the

---

[118] "When We All Get to Heaven." E.E. Hewitt (1898).
[119] N.T. Wright, "Heaven Is Not Our Home."

most important aspects of the Christian faith? The answer to the first question is no. No, I am not rejecting the afterlife. The answer to the second question is yes. Yes, I realize that it is one of the most important aspects of the Christian faith. More than that, I would suggest that it is the very most important aspect of our faith. If there is no afterlife, there is no purpose or meaning in life. At least, not ultimately. We know this both logically and scripturally. Anyone who is being honest knows that the events of our lives are fleeting, and that they will disappear along with us at death. At best, everything has limited meaning. The greatness of any moment vanishes the minute it is over, if nothing survives our mortality. I have talked to many atheists who disagree, but they have no leg to stand on. Sadly, they know this. Paul stated the futility of the situation perfectly: "If we have hoped in Christ in this life only, we are of all men most to be pitied" (1 Cor. 15:19). Pitied, yes. It would be bad enough to live for a lie, but much worse to attempt to lead selfless and charitable lives—which Christians are called to do—when there would be no purpose in doing so. If nothing awaits us—no crown of glory, or anything of the sort—then we would have sacrificed so much for so little. Well, for *nothing*, really.

Clearly, I could not be a bigger proponent of the necessity of the afterlife. It is the nature of the afterlife, however, that is in question. It would be very difficult to find a single person who has not been assured by someone that heaven is awaiting those who believe in God. At this point, it simply goes without saying within most parts of the church (and outside of it, for that matter). I understand the emotional needs this satisfies. There is perhaps nothing more comforting than to hear that our deceased loved ones are "looking down on us from heaven," and that they are in a "better place." Cliché, yes: but satisfying nonetheless. However, this is only true on the surface. At first blush, it sounds appealing to think of our deceased loved ones as now residing in heaven. When probed at all, legitimate issues begin to emerge.

At some point—if we are serious about taking this line of thinking to its logical end—we must ask a very important question: would we want our mothers, fathers, brothers, sisters, spouses, friends, or—Lord forbid—our children, seeing what happens in our lives after they are gone? It's appealing to think that they might be celebrating with us at, say, our college graduation, our wedding, or at the news of a big job promotion. But we also must consider what that sort of ability (the ability to see our lives) would also bring with it. Every time we fall short; every time we fail; every time we lash out at others in anger; every time we suffer; every time we make others suffer; every time we sin; every time that tragedy strikes; and every time that someone passes away . . . they would be watching.

Would your mom or dad want to watch you die? Would we want them to have to do that? What about a deceased spouse or a lost child: would it be good for them to observe our mental and physical degradation and, ultimately, our deaths? These questions should be read rhetorically—no one in their right mind would want that. The issue worsens when we consider that the same concept would apply to every other aspect of our lives. If the dead are truly "watching over us from heaven," then they are seeing all of it: the good, the bad, and the ugly. I have personally spoken with both widows and widowers who were incredibly uncomfortable with the idea that their spouses were still hanging around in some way or observing their actions. I have even known people who refused to get married for the duration of their lives, solely because they could not bear to disappoint (or even frustrate) their deceased husbands or wives. Connected to all this is another serious problem: wouldn't the ability to see everything that is going on in our world essentially equate to having God-like knowledge and understanding? Isn't it God—and God alone—who is supposed to be able to peer into every person's life, and track his or her every move? It troubles me that most of us are so eager to grant those abilities to deceased human beings. It should bother those of us who do it.

God can handle this ability—but even He mourns our losses; "Costly in the sight of the Lord is the death of His saints" (Ps. 116:15).

We of course know that Jesus wept at the death of his friend Lazarus (Jn. 11:35). However, it is incredibly presumptuous to believe that deceased human beings can endure seeing all the death and suffering that occurs in our world. And then, what type of "heavenly" existence would that even be? That doesn't sound like a place of bliss to me. With these issues in mind, it is only fair to note that not everyone holds to these views. In my personal experience—based on what I have heard others within the church both say and teach—the overwhelming majority of those who believe that the righteous depart to heaven at death also believe that these individuals are able to observe (or even influence) the living.

However, one might subscribe to the view that people go to heaven when they die, but that they are not able to know what goes on in our world at that time. In a sense, God shields them from seeing the tragic elements of the world, since being able to see them would not align with the world of bliss that heaven is thought to be. If accurate, they certainly aren't watching over us from heaven, so we can immediately throw that idea out. Further, there isn't a single verse in the sixty-six books of the Bible that would back up this claim; it's just wishful thinking. As a final point related to this line of reasoning, consider what it means for the living. We can speculate endlessly about where our loved ones are and what they are doing. Prayers for the dead are an extremely common practice for many believers (particularly in the Roman Catholic faith), and "ghost hunting" has seen incredibly popularity over the last twenty years, both within the U.S. and in many other parts of the world. As I previously mentioned,[120] these practices are completely off limits within the Bible. Believers are strongly prohibited from making any effort to contact the dead, and such practices always end up in an unholy place. The spirits of deceased believers are not there to interact with us, but other forces certainly are.

---

[120] See the section, "Unseen Forces" in chapter two.

If we transition further away from the logical issues and look at the matter from a scriptural perspective, we find further reason to cast doubt on the standard belief in dying and going to heaven. At the bare minimum, the Bible does not focus on heaven as the goal of the afterlife. At the most, it offers few substantive reasons to believe that we will ever go to heaven. In the Bible, heaven is the abode of God and the angels. There is heaven, and there is earth. While the two were intended to intermingle in very fluid ways, human beings were not created to live in heaven, but to live on earth. Nowhere in Scripture is it evident that we were intended to live on earth, *and then* live in heaven. God has something much bigger in mind, which I will later return to discussing. Instead, death represents a period of unconsciousness: a time of "sleep," as the biblical figures often called it. From the teachings of the prophet Daniel, to the writings of the apostles, to the words of Christ himself, death is consistently compared to sleep.

When speaking of the resurrection, the prophet Daniel said: "Many of those who sleep in the dust of the ground will awake, these to everlasting life, but the others to disgrace and everlasting contempt" (12:2). Concerning his own future, Daniel was given this directive: "But as for you, go your way to the end; then you will enter into rest and rise again for your allotted portion at the end of the age" (12:13). That would be a reference to the resurrection, not a disembodied interim period. When discussing the millennial glory of those who had been martyred, the book of Revelation clearly echoes Daniel's sentiment, saying: "They came to life and reigned with Christ a thousand years" (20:4). The Greek word used for "came to life" (*ezēsan*) displays the fact that these individuals were not previously living, since one cannot come back to life if they are already alive. As though they were asleep, they "woke up."

In perhaps the most persuasive passage of the Bible regarding the sleep-death parallel, Paul made it as clear as possible that believers will live again *at the resurrection* and not before then:

"But we do not want you to be uninformed, brethren, about those who are asleep, so that you will not grieve as do the rest who have no hope. For if we believe that Jesus died and rose again, even so God will bring with Him those who have fallen asleep in Jesus. For this we say to you by the word of the Lord, that we who are alive and remain until the coming of the Lord, will not precede those who have fallen asleep. For the Lord Himself will descend from heaven with a shout, with the voice of the archangel and with the trumpet of God, and the dead in Christ will rise first. Then we who are alive and remain will be caught up together with them in the clouds to meet the Lord in the air, and so we shall always be with the Lord. Therefore comfort one another with these words" (1 Thes. 4:13-18).

The most striking aspect of these teachings is that the church at Thessalonica had specifically asked Paul about this issue. They had questioned Paul about the fate of those who had died prior to the return of Christ, since many had done so by then and the Lord had not yet returned. Rather than telling them that the dead are already living with Christ, Paul took this opportunity to say something quite different. He noted that death should be compared to sleep, rather than some heightened sense of awareness. More importantly, he specified when the dead would "wake up" from their slumber: at Jesus' return. Then, *and only then*, the voice of the archangel and the trumpet of God will call them forth. Clearly, this message is not consistent with the standard belief in dying and going to heaven.

The sleep-death comparison also shows up when Jesus raised a synagogue leaders' daughter back to life (Mt. 9:24), and when he described Lazarus' condition: "Our friend Lazarus has fallen asleep; but I go, so that I may awaken him out of sleep" (Jn. 11:11). Just to drive the comparison home, it is worth noting that the apostles—true to their often-bewildered form—responded to Jesus, saying, "Lord, if he has fallen asleep, he will recover" (11:12). The text does not specifically tell us who said this to

Jesus, but the smart money is on Peter! Thankfully, the narrator (John) was quick to clear this up for the audience: "Now Jesus had spoken of his death, but they thought that He was speaking of literal sleep" (11:13). Another telling example is right before Stephen—the first Christian martyr—was stoned to death. Immediately before his passing, Acts reveals his final moments: "Then falling on his knees, he cried out with a loud voice, 'Lord, do not hold this sin against them!' Having said this, he fell asleep" (7:60). There are many other instances that prove the sleep-death parallel, but this should be established by now. However, the question remains as to *why* these ideas are connected within the Bible. Elsewhere,[121] I have explained the reasons for this correlation, but I will summarize them here:

1) Both are unconscious modes of existence.

2) Both are characterized by the absence of temporal recognition.

3) Both are merely temporary in nature.

This is intended to suggest that death is compared to sleep because we are unaware of what happens during both, we have no understanding of time during both, and both will ultimately end when we awaken from our slumber.

There are a couple issues here that must also be addressed. Paul spoke of Christ's return and the resurrection as the time when the dead would live again, and this theme is consistent throughout the Bible. However, what sense would a world-changing event like the resurrection make if the dead were already living in heaven (or elsewhere)? The entire concept of resurrection is explicitly about being *raised back* to life, and in bodily form. One cannot be resurrected if they are already living any more than someone can be cured if they are already well. Disembodied life during the interim period renders the resurrection pointless.

---

[121] *The Death Myth*, 22-23.

In addition to this, a conscious interim existence also destroys the purpose of another prominent biblical theme: the great Day of Judgment. Jesus spoke of the Judgment in his Parable of the Weeds (or Tares), found in Matthew 13:24-43. There, he clearly stated that the righteous and the wicked would only be separated at the "harvest;" that is, when Christ will return with his angels, in order to separate the righteous from the wicked. This theme goes all the way back to the writings of the prophets, when they discussed the concept of the "day of the Lord" (Joel 1:15) and the judgment it will involve. In the New Testament, this was called the "day of the Lord Jesus" (2 Cor. 1:14), and also the "day of Christ" (Phil. 1:10). Other places where the concept of the Judgment shows up are in the book of Daniel (12:2), Paul's second letter to the Thessalonians (1:5-10), and Revelation 20, just to name a few. The Judgment is a fundamental biblical doctrine. The problem is that it too becomes pointless if all of the deceased have already been judged at death. In order for God to sentence individuals to either a place of bliss or a place of torment, He would have to evaluate their lives and make a *judgment* on the matter. This type of act has been called Particular Judgment, and it suggests that God will decide each person's ultimate fate at the moment they die, rather than at the resurrection. If Particular Judgment is true, then the great Day of Judgment is utterly unnecessary.

As another argument to consider, recall the earlier point that neither Satan nor the demons are living in hell at the present time. This is incredibly important, since they are the very beings it was chiefly designed for (Mt. 25:41)! When we factor in that the righteous and the wicked will not be separated until Christ's return, we arrive at the fact that deceased individuals are not currently dwelling somewhere. If the dead are not living in hell, then they are not living in heaven either. A final matter must be quickly addressed, since it is extremely relevant to this discussion. The issue involves the resurrection body. Paul referred to the bodies we will receive at Christ's return as "spiritual bodies" (1 Cor. 15:44). I will evaluate this in much greater detail throughout the next couple sections of the book, but for now it is important to note that the spiritual bodies will be an upgrade to our current bodies in every imaginable way (15:42-45). This being the case, we simply must ask about the purpose of being given bodies at the resurrection. If, during the interim period, we will indeed be able to live as disembodied spirits, why would we need to have bodies at the resurrection? If we want to be realistic about it, why do we even need the bodies we have now? The typical Christian view of the afterlife renders this body—and the resurrection body—wholly unnecessary.

Two more problems arise when we consider the nature of the soul that is alleged to dwell inside of (or attached to) us. First, the issue of ensoulment has been around since people began to think about the concept of the soul, and it is not likely to ever disappear. When and how each of us is given a soul is impossible to square with the traditional view of an "immortal soul." This essentially holds that the soul is an immaterial "us" that resides within the body, then persists apart from it after death. But does God simply create a blank soul—devoid of all personality—at some point after conception, as "creationism" holds? Is the soul the product of physical procreation, as "traducianism" suggests? If the former is true, is God there to insert a soul into a child conceived by rape, incest, or even through something like artificial insemination? To put it mildly, these would be very sticky situations to attach God to. Further, having a soul would not be necessary for human life. If the person can live (in the womb) for some unknown period without a soul, what is the purpose of the soul? Why add it to the mix? If the soul is the product of natural procreation, as traducianism advocates, how could we really conceive (pardon the pun) of such a thing? The union of the *physical* sperm and egg somehow results in an *immaterial* soul? That doesn't quite compute. Sure, we can throw our hands up and attribute these views to the "mysteries of God." The problem is that we could validate almost any other view of ensoulment with this type of handwaving; it simply isn't helpful. As rational beings, we must do our best to make sense of difficult issues, not gloss over them. Clearly, ensoulment is a major hurdle to jump if we are to believe in a soul that will one day live on its own.

The second major problem is what we might call "soul damage." We have all heard of those who suffered brain damage from a critical blow to the head, but if you think about it, the same types of injuries would also have to change the soul. When one receives brain damage, particularly of the severe variety, their personality changes. Who the person was prior to their head injury is often not the same as who they are afterwards. I recall a good childhood friend, and the horrific car accident his mother endured during our youth. The results were devastating, to put it mildly. His mother went from being an attractive, intelligent, and charismatic individual, to being a perpetual child *in an instant*. She lost her adult thinking capacities, and even her appearance drastically changed after the traumatic brain injury she received. This type of phenomenon simply doesn't square with typical understandings of the soul. If the soul is the immaterial "us" that resides in the body—it guides the body, makes the decisions, does the contemplation, etc.—then why should a physical injury affect it? Shouldn't the soul be immune to physical damage? Of course, this is a catch-22. On the one hand, it is illogical to think that an immaterial soul would be altered by what happens to the physical body. On the other, if our souls are not affected by what happens throughout our physical lives, then the soul cannot be the source of our identities; it would never change, and there could not be any personal growth or character development. This challenge should tell us that the soul is not what it is popularly believed to be. Not surprisingly, the Bible illustrates that the body and the soul are intertwined and do not function apart from one another. Put another way, we do not *have* souls; we *are* souls. The reason physical injuries affect our entire being is that there is not a "ghost in the machine."

We are now able to summarize these perspectives. If one chooses to believe that we will go on to live as disembodied spirits during the interim period—the time between death and the resurrection—they would also have to battle the following dilemmas: 1) The resurrection is redundant if the dead already live; 2) The Day of Judgment is unnecessary, since the dead have already been judged; 3) The separation of the righteous and the wicked is superfluous, because it has already occurred; 4) The resurrection body is a needless addition to an otherwise functioning being; and 5) This view suffers tremendously from the issue of ensoulment and the concept of "soul damage." As if all this weren't enough, one would need to explain away the obvious connections between sleep and death. Dying and "going to heaven" looks less and less to be the case. This is true from both a logical and a biblical perspective. However, that does not mean there are no examples one could point to in order to try and substantiate this view. Since there are relatively few passages in this group, I will briefly assess the most referenced ones here and now.

The most quoted passage of Scripture that is used to support disembodied existence during the interim period might well be the Parable of the Rich Man and Lazarus, found in Luke 16:19-31. In truth, I find this example to strain credibility more than most of the others, so it is curious as to why it is so used in this capacity. In this passage, Jesus tells a story about two men and how their lives played out both in life and after death. The rich man is depicted as being callous and corrupt, and Lazarus is described as an exceedingly poor (but righteous) man. Lazarus begged— like the dogs that came to lick his wounds—the rich man for help, but the rich man consistently ignored his requests. Clearly, the two men had very different situations while on earth; one was healthy, wealthy, and prosperous, while the other was ill and impoverished. That all changed after death, as Jesus explained. At that time, Lazarus went to a place of comfort called "Abraham's bosom," and the rich man went to a place of torment called "Hades." The script had totally flipped, and their fortunes had been reversed. There is a powerful dialogue that takes place as the story unfolds, and it has some very important teaching points about living for God now (rather than later), and what type of evidence would be sufficient for belief in God. For our purposes, the important part is that both men were said to have gone on to a type of afterlife immediately after death. Since they did, it is often believed that we will too. In other words, Jesus was trying to tell us that the same options await us when we die.

There are numerous problems with this interpretation. First and foremost, *this story is a parable*; that is, it is a fictional story intended to illustrate a deeper point about God, faith, morality, or a number of other topics. We know this is a parable for several reasons. For starters, the Rich Man and Lazarus is placed within a larger framework of other parables. In Luke's gospel, this story follows a string of others which are all clearly parables. Directly preceding this tale, we see the Parable of the Shrewd Manager (16:1-15). Before that, the Parable of the Prodigal Son (15:11-32). Those stories begin with the introductions, "there was a rich man" and "there was a man." The Rich Man and Lazarus follows suit, beginning with the line "there was a rich man." Clearly, these accounts have storybook or teaching tale introductions. But what comes before the Prodigal Son? Not surprisingly, we find that the parables of the Lost Sheep (15:1-7) and the Lost Coin (15:8-10) do. Are you noticing a pattern here?

This brings us to the next issue: only one of the two main characters were given names. It has long been suggested that we should interpret the Rich Man and Lazarus differently because one of the characters is named. The rationale is that real names are seldom attached to fictional accounts, so naming the character Lazarus indicates that the story must be historically true. While quarrelling with those who believed that death represents an unconscious state ("soul sleep"), John Calvin once remarked:

> "Let them produce even one passage from Scripture where anyone is called by name in a parable! What is meant by the words - 'There was a poor man named Lazarus?' Either the Word of God must lie, or it is a true narrative."[122]

152

As I mentioned, the immediate issue with this reasoning is that the other character is unnamed. Since the rich man was not given a proper name, shouldn't we conclude that he was not a real person? In truth, there are plenty of other characters who were not given names in Scripture (like Lot's wife and Noah's daughters-in-law) that we still believe were real people. Likewise, there are characters who were given names (like Eliphaz, Bildad, Zophar and Elihu) that many interpreters do not believe were real.[123] This leads to the final point, which is that the Rich Man and Lazarus is chock-full of colorful imagery that we would normally associate with parables. The use of Hades (which was a Greek idea about a shadowy underground labyrinth for souls), Abraham's side, the great chasm, and the agonizing fire, all prove this. It is simply unrealistic to use the Parable of the Rich Man and Lazarus as evidence of a literal afterlife.

Another passage that is typically used to prove that the righteous dead go to heaven is Jesus' interaction with the criminal on the cross, in Luke 23:39-43. I will say at the forefront that this is a more compelling example than the last. Here, both Jesus and a man who was guilty of crimes against the Roman Empire—which was what normally caused someone to endure crucifixion—are having a discussion as they painfully await their deaths. Unlike the other criminal present, the man Jesus is talking to defends Jesus' integrity, and asks that he be remembered when he comes into his kingdom (23:42). This display of faith prompts Jesus to respond favorably, saying, "Truly I say to you, today you will be with Me in Paradise." This has caused many to believe that both Jesus and the criminal were going to depart to heaven after the horrible crucifixion process had run its course.

---

[122] John Calvin, *Tracts & Letters – Psychopannychia*.

[123] The overall case for the fictional nature of the story of Job is very sound. Almost nothing about it can be pinned down to history, and most of its features are highly allegorical. Refer to Crenshaw's *Old Testament Wisdom* (pg. 16) for more information on the matter.

However, there is a distinct possibility that we should read Jesus' words a bit differently. As it is normally translated, there is a comma present before the word "today." However, it could actually be that the comma should be placed *after* the word "today." No such punctuation marks existed in the early manuscripts, and it is left to the translators to decide where these should be placed. Clearly, moving the comma would have enormous implications. This would be the difference between Jesus telling the man they were going to Paradise *that very day*, and him saying that they would *someday* do so. Because the man asked Jesus to remember him when he returned in his kingdom, it is reasonable to believe that Jesus was affirming that he would (rather than that very day). On the other hand, it is fair to say that most of the occasions where Jesus says, "Truly I tell you . . ." within the gospels, the comma would logically go after the word "you." The comma issue is at best inconclusive, but it is important to note that the passage may not read as it is normally translated.

A deeper question concerns the place they would be going: Paradise. In certain rabbinic traditions, Paradise was viewed as the place of bliss that man had lost through the Fall. Over time, it came to be viewed by some as the place for fallen saints.[124] This is how most commentators view Jesus' discussion with the criminal on the cross, but there are issues with this. Paradise (*paradeisos*) is an enigmatic term in the NT, as it is used only three times in its entirety. Besides the passage at hand in Luke, it is used in 2 Corinthians 12:4, and in Revelation 2:7. As mentioned in the section "Sky Beings," Paul used this term when he discussed his trip to the "third heaven," which is synonymous with Paradise in that passage. There, the term was used to describe the farthest part of the heavens, where God Himself was thought to reside. However, Revelation's use of this term is entirely different. It reads as follows: "He who has an ear, let him hear what the Spirit says to the churches. To him who overcomes, I will grant to eat of the tree of life which is in the Paradise of God" (2:7).

---

[124] H.A. Kent Jr., "Paradise," 891.

The "Paradise of God" hearkens back to the ideal state that Adam and Eve found themselves in before they rebelled. More than looking back, however, Revelation is actually looking forward to the time when the world will return to its intended state of order. In essence, Paradise was about the world that is to come.

So, what did Paradise typically refer to in the Bible? The short answer is that we cannot be entirely sure. Certainly, the term displays some flexibility. Of its three occurrences, it is used at least two different ways. Revelation uses it to discuss the future return to the type of world God had originally intended, and Paul described it as a place above or beyond the heavens. In theory, Jesus could have been referring to either option. However, it may make better sense if Jesus was using this term as Revelation does. The criminal wanted to be there when Jesus returned and ushered in the new world, which is precisely how Paradise is used in Revelation. If anything, this perhaps suggests that the comma should go after the word "today," and that Luke 23:43 is about the return of Christ and the finished Kingdom of God, not some disembodied existence that takes place between this life and the resurrection.

The final point is that, even if the criminal and Jesus went some place after death, this would not tell us much about what awaits us. Like Elijah and Enoch's ascensions or Moses' appearance at the Transfiguration, the criminal's experience cannot be taken to apply as the general rule for everyone who dies. These are unique scenarios, not instructions about what will occur. If you want a passage of Scripture that would fit such a bill, look no further than the aforementioned 1 Thessalonians 4:13-18. That was given as *general* instruction to the church in Thessalonica and, by extension, to any believer who reads the letter. It is very important that we make a distinction between events that are recorded and things that we are supposed to apply to our own lives. In this case, the record that an event happened (if it indeed happened *that day*) to the man on the cross does not speak to what we should expect. Instead, we should look to those instances where people were given a direct teaching on the matter.

Another text that often comes up with regards to the afterlife is Philippians 1:22-24. There, Paul mulls over whether it would be better to leave this world or continue because of his role with the churches:

> "For to me, to live is Christ and to die is gain. But if I am to live on in the flesh, this will mean fruitful labor for me; and I do not know which to choose. But I am hard-pressed from both directions, having the desire to depart and be with Christ, for that is very much better; yet to remain on in the flesh is more necessary for your sake."

It is often thought that the dilemma Paul is describing is about whether to stay alive on earth or to die, leaving his "flesh" in order to go live in heaven. But upon closer inspection, it becomes clear that this is *not* what he actually intended. One reason is that the word Paul used ("flesh") had a range of meanings, but here it referred to the reality of living with a fallen body in a fallen world. This was about leaving the broken world and being prepared for the restored creation; this was not about his soul leaving the body to live in an immaterial realm. Linked to this, there is another reason that involves Paul's overall worldview and his understanding of what would occur after death. As I explained with 1 Thessalonians 4:13-18, he had a very clear picture of what awaits believers. When Christ returns and wakes the dead, they will then live again. Paul understood all this in terms of Christ's return (the "Parousia") and the culmination of human history. As he saw things, leaving this world is to instantaneously "be with Christ," since the next conscious thing we will experience after death is Jesus' return. Again, he laid this out plainly to the Thessalonians who specifically asked him about it.

Perhaps the most convincing reason why Paul was not talking about dying and going to heaven is what he offers within the same letter. For example, Paul says that "on the day of Christ" he will "have reason to glory" because of the faithfulness of the believers in Philippi (2:16). Concerning himself, Paul expressed that his hope was to "know Him and the power of His resurrection," in order that he "may attain to the

156

resurrection from the dead" (3:10-11). His entire mindset about the afterlife revolved around the resurrection, not a disembodied interim period. More strongly, Paul adds the following:

> "For our citizenship is in heaven, from which we eagerly wait for a Savior, the Lord Jesus Christ; who will the body of our humble state into conformity with the body of His Glory, by the exertion of the power that He has even to subject all things to Himself" (3:20-21).

While we are indeed children of heaven, that is not our future. Instead, we "eagerly await" Christ's return, so we can receive a body the likes of which Christ received at the Resurrection. This notion is certainly not confined to Philippians either; it is a consistent theme in Paul's writings. He adds further clarification to this in passages like Colossians 3:4 and 2 Timothy 4:6-8.[125] At the end of the day, Paul would have royally contradicted himself if his intention in Philippians 1:22-24 was to suggest that he would die and go live in heaven as a disembodied being. That would not align with the overall content of the letter, nor would it mesh with what he told other churches and individuals. Furthermore, it would differ from the teachings of Jesus himself.

Beyond these passages, there are few others that are *frequently* referenced to support the idea that human beings die and then consciously live somewhere prior to the resurrection. Typically, there is handwaving about some of the Psalms[126] and certain parts of Revelation (like 6:9-11).

---

[125] Colossians 3:4 reads, "When Christ, who is our life, is revealed, then you also will be revealed with Him in glory." 2 Timothy 4:8 says, ". . . in the future there is laid up for me the crown of righteousness, which the Lord, the righteous Judge, will award to me on that day; and not only to me, but also to all who have loved His appearing." Both examples place the afterlife squarely in terms of Christ's return.

[126] Psalms 55:15, 88:11-12, and 139:8 are examples of this. However, there are Psalms that directly contradict this notion. Consider two examples: 88:5 tells us that the dead are "cut off" from God and forgotten, and 115:17 says, "The dead do not praise the LORD, Nor do any who go down into silence." As a whole, the Psalms actually portray the grave (*Sheol*) as a place of silence and inactivity which, of

These are very weak arguments, however, since the poetic and figurative styles of these passages is undeniable. Like the Parable of the Rich Man and Lazarus, such examples are not intended to be taken as literal descriptions of what happens (or what *has* happened) to human beings after death. Adding weight to this issue is that the entire premise of using texts like the Rich Man and Lazarus, the criminal on the cross, Paul's words in Philippians 1:22-24, and certain passages within Psalms and Revelation—all as common evidence about the afterlife—is extremely problematic. The reason why is simple: these passages do not point towards the same realities. For instance, the Parable of the Rich Man and Lazarus talks about "Abraham's bosom" and "Hades" as the two destinations for the deceased. Meanwhile, the account of the criminal on the cross and Philippians 1:22-24 are believed to be about going to heaven. The problem is that Abraham's bosom, Hades, Paradise, as well as heaven and hell, are unquestionably not the same things. This being the case, there is no rational justification for smashing them all together and pretending that they are. The blessed deceased could potentially go to heaven, or to Abraham's bosom, or to Paradise, but not some combination of these. Likewise, the unrepentant might go to Hades or to hell, but they most certainly will not go to both destinations. Like ammonia and bleach, the normative view of the afterlife is a cocktail of ingredients that simply shouldn't be mixed.

The information I have provided here is merely a summation of what is a highly complex issue. There are other ideas and passages of Scripture that pertain to this matter, but it would take an entire book to properly cover them. As it turns out, I have actually written just such a text. For those who are interested in a much more thorough perspective on what the Bible has to say about the afterlife, I refer you to *The Death Myth*. Having said this, it should be clear that the standard view that people die and immediately go to either a place of bliss or a place of

course, it is.

punishment is at best misguided, and at worst completely misunderstood. Based on the contents of this section, I am aware that the "apple cart" has been thoroughly upset. Any reader would be well within their rights to ask what the alternative is. If heaven is not the end of our story, what is? If heaven is not the afterlife—it is not the hope, the dream, or the goal of the Christian faith—what on earth is? As I mentioned earlier, God has something much bigger in mind for us. But not just for us: for the heavenly beings as well.

God on Earth

One of the most astonishing features of the Bible is its arrangement. It presents us with sixty-six books that collectively span thousands of years of history, cut across dozens of cultures and languages, involve far more authors than we are even aware of, and cover almost every range of literary genres. This miraculous text seamlessly weaves poetry and metaphor with historical narrative and fact. When considering the incredible diversity of thought and influence contained within its pages, it seems impossible that it could tell a completely connected story about God's dealings with humanity. But it does; it most certainly does. Scripture takes us through a series of highs and lows, peaks and valleys, and victories and defeats. It takes the reader on an historic journey through the ancient world and, in particular, it discusses the life of a people who are collectively called "Israel." This story spans from Creation, to the Exodus, to the period of judges and kings, to the exile and its prophetic minds, to Jesus, to the life of the early church, to what to expect at the end of the age, and so much more. In all this, it preserves a continuity that should frankly be impossible. Without God, it certainly would be.

It is really the beginning and end of the story that are the most consequential at present: how it all started, and how it will all end.

Incredibly—and by design, no doubt—the Bible concludes in much the same way as it begins. In Genesis 1-2, we read about the world God intended for us: the way it *ought* to have been. This was a "good" creation; "God saw all that He had made, and behold, it was very good" (1:31). Some are quick to point out that "very good" does not mean "perfect," or anything of the sort. In fact, it has become dogma among those of the evolutionary creationism ilk (formerly "theistic evolution") that Creation was flawed (though they seldom *directly* claim as much) at its inception. This being the case, the world is not "fallen" in any normal sense of the term. Everything we see around us was intended by God and was indeed part of His "good Creation." In his attempt to harmonize evolutionary theory with biblical teaching, theoretical physicist John Polkinghorne explains to us how we can make sense of suffering and evil within the world:

> "God has self-limited divine power by allowing the other truly to be itself. The gift of Love must be the gift of freedom . . . It is the nature of lions that they seek their prey. It is the nature of cells that they will mutate, sometimes producing cancers. It is the nature of humankind that sometimes people will act with selfishness. That these things are so is not gratuitous or due to divine oversight or indifference. They are the necessary cost of a creation given by its Creator the freedom to be itself."[127]

We should appreciate anyone who is willing to try their hand at explaining the issue of theodicy, but the conclusion that God *intended* harmful mutations, cancers, and, by extension, death, is inescapable on this view. Within the world of evolutionary creationism, we can reject the Fall of Man, the entrance of sin into the world, the historical existence of Adam and Eve, and a variety of vital biblical doctrines. This is a worldview that relies upon the creation of the living world by a virtually absent Creator,[128]

---

[127] John Polkinghorne, *Belief in God in an Age of Science*, 13.

[128] This mentality is masterfully displayed in Wayne Rossiter's, *Shadow of Oz: Theistic*

who passively allows the biosphere the "freedom" to create itself through destructive processes: methods producing results that we would normally associate with suffering or evil. But this is nothing short of pure hokum. This applies to the general perspective, and specifically to the view that Creation was intended to be completed in a tarnished state.

Genesis records that the entirety of Creation was not just "good" (*towb*), but "very good" (*meod; towb*). This is an emphatic way of talking about what God had made. Creation was exceedingly good, and there is not a particularly stronger way to have said it. When *meod* is used as an adverb throughout the OT, it intensifies the word associated with it. Cain became *very* angry when God rejected his sacrifice (Gen. 4:5). Abraham's wife, Sarah, was *very* beautiful (Gen. 12:14). Joshua and Caleb reported that the land of Canaan was *exceedingly* good (Num. 14:7). This expression connotes things that aren't simply decent or acceptable but are over and above the quality of comparable things (other women, other lands, etc.). This should reveal to us that God did not create a fallen, broken, or even scarred world. It only became that way later on. Overall, the entire case that God did not make a "perfect" creation is both highly subjective and *purposely* misleading. What does one mean by the word "perfect?" When most Christians use this term to explain Creation, they mean to imply that it was not corrupted; there was no sin, suffering, death, etc., at least as these things pertain to human beings. They do not mean some highly philosophical concept of an incomprehensible state of perfection. For this reason (and others) the argument is a red herring. It is a way to change the landscape of the conversation in order to score a cheap theological point, while also opening a path to the type of agenda promoted by evolutionary creationism.

Evolution and the Absent God. The same could be said of Matti Leisola's, *Heretic: One Scientist's Journey from Darwin to Design.* For those interested in investigating the connections between evolutionary theory and biblical teaching, I highly recommend these resources.

As the Bible describes things, it was Adam and Eve's rebellion—based on their trust in the serpent's advice—that caused Creation to deteriorate from its *meod; towb* ("very good") state of existence. This was the entrance of sin into the world of humans (not of angels), and it was in many respects an example of paradise lost. After Genesis 3, almost everything recorded in Scripture concerns the plan to fix things: to get back to paradise and the very good world that was created. As it turns out, the Bible ends with a beautiful vision of this kind of world. John was given a glimpse into a time when heaven and earth will once again coexist harmoniously:

> "Then I saw a new heaven and a new earth; for the first heaven and the first earth passed away, and there is no longer any sea. And I saw the holy city, new Jerusalem, coming down out of heaven from God, made ready as a bride adorned for her husband. And I heard a loud voice from the throne, saying, 'Behold, the tabernacle of God is among men, and He will dwell among them, and they shall be His people, and God Himself will be among them, and He will wipe away every tear from their eyes; and there will no longer be any death; there will no longer be any mourning, or crying, or pain; the first things have passed away.' And He who sits on the throne said, 'Behold, I am making all things new'" (21:1-5).

Here, we have the concept of a new creation: a glance back at Genesis 1-2, but a simultaneous glance into a time not yet experienced by John or even us. A glowing city emerges from the heavens and, with it, a world devoid of our greatest struggles. Death, mourning, pain and despair are no longer the law of the land, for those things have passed away.

For the sake of the current topic, the last part of chapter twenty-one is the most important. There, John recorded the final union of God and humankind:

"I saw no temple in it, for the Lord God the Almighty and the Lamb are its temple. And the city has no need of the sun or of the moon to shine on it, for the glory of God has illumined it, and its lamp is the Lamb. The nations will walk by its light, and the kings of the earth will bring their glory into it. In the daytime (for there will be no night there) its gates will never be closed; and they will bring the glory and the honor of the nations into it; and nothing unclean, and no one who practices abomination and lying, shall ever come into it, but only those whose names are written in the Lamb's book of life" (21:22-27).

When these two passages are put together, a stunning reality emerges. Think about two lines, in particular: "Behold, the tabernacle of God is among men, and He will dwell among them," and "I saw no temple in it, for the Lord God the Almighty and the Lamb are its temple." In the OT, God commanded the Israelites to create a large, portable tent that would allow God's presence to travel with them through the wilderness (Ex. 36-38). They called this marvel "the tabernacle." In some sense, one could understand the tabernacle as a moving temple: a foreshadowing of the stationary masterpiece that King Solomon would later build for God.

It is no coincidence that the same John who is traditionally believed to have written Revelation recorded something very similar about Jesus, when he walked the earth. Though our translations of John 1:14 usually say that Jesus "dwelt among us," that word (*skénoó*) most literally means to dwell "as in a tent," to "encamp," or even to "tabernacle."[129] Jesus *tabernacled* among us. Now, at the end of our age, we see this idea come up once more. This time, however, there is a twist. Rather than there being a physical structure to house God's presence, we have God living right there among His people. There will be no need for a temple; "the Lord God the Almighty and the Lamb are its temple."

---

[129] Strong's Greek Concordance, 4637 "skénoó."

This is a truly masterful motif, and it runs throughout the biblical narrative. But we cannot forget where this idea started: in the Garden of Eden. This began at Creation. We read in Genesis that God once walked among Adam and Eve in the garden (3:8). On top of these major occasions when God lived (or will live) among human beings, there were various points where God physically showed up to His people. If you remember from earlier in the book, I discussed when God spoke with Moses "face to face, just as a man speaks to his friend" (Ex. 33:11). Afterwards, God passed by Moses but did not allow him to see His full glory (Ex. 33:18-23). God famously wrestled with Jacob (Gen. 32:24-32). God walked on earth before the Fall, visited His people throughout the OT, and ultimately united with humanity through Jesus so that He could walk among us on earth. When Christ returns to create the new heaven and new earth, God will walk with us once more. At that point, existence will be set right. We will have returned to Eden, but perhaps even exceeded its splendor. It is important to incorporate one more biblical scene, which was covered in the previous section of the book. Paul described the great hope of the afterlife as being the day that Jesus returns to earth with his angels. On that day, the trumpet will blast, the dead will awaken, and all believers will reign with Christ (1 Thes. 4:13-18). All these passages show us something vital—truly imperative—about the God's Kingdom and His intentions in creating human beings. Hopefully, you are seeing the trend here.

The bottom line is this: with all our talk about getting to heaven, the Bible reveals that the goal is exactly the opposite. *Entirely, completely, and utterly,* the opposite. We do not go to God; God comes to us. Mortal man does not travel to heaven; the "heavenly man" travels to earth. We do not ascend to meet the angels; the angels descend to meet us. These things reflect the biblical narrative and point us towards its goal. God, the angels, and transformed human beings will inhabit the same world. Of course, there is more to this grand hope than living together. The full scope of the project will be to share in a new creation. The new heavens and new earth: that is the great expectation.

In this, we are clearly talking about a world that does not carry the flaws of our fallen existence. But what exactly will this look like? There are two predominant answers to that question. The first is that the new heavens and new earth is a wholly new creation, and all of existence will essentially be remade. In particular, the letters traditionally attributed to the apostle Peter provide reason to believe this. There, it describes the destruction of this current world at Christ's return: "But the day of the Lord will come like a thief. The heavens will disappear with a roar; the elements will be destroyed by fire, and the earth and everything done in it will be laid bare" (2 Pet. 3:10). Immediately after this fiery pronouncement, the letter clarifies exactly why God will destroy the earth: ". . . we are looking for new heavens and a new earth, in which righteousness dwells" (3:13). However, this idea preceded the letters of Peter by many hundreds of years. At the beginning of what scholars have called the "Little Apocalypse" (cc. 24-27), Isaiah described that God will completely plunder the earth and devastate it (24:1). This theme shows up throughout Isaiah, but it culminates in a familiar hope: a new heaven and a new earth (65:17 and 66:22).

The alternative would be that God does not create a whole new world from scratch, but that He transforms or renews our world into something much more magnificent. The central idea of transformation is that something (or someone) is taken from its current form and changed into something greater. Given this reality, and the often-metaphorical nature of the texts that describe a totally new creation, some have concluded that God is not literally going to destroy everything we see and start over. Instead, these texts are alluding to the overarching belief that the next world will be new and improved. While the biblical case favors the literal approach, this is an area of little consequence to us. Either way, the new creation will be a place of great splendor that will not leave any of us wanting.

With the contents of this section in mind, I perceive our whole existence as something like a beautiful painting. This painting, however, was not properly cared for and was even purposely tarnished at points. Over time, it became something less than its former self. Its colors have faded a bit, and its accents are covered with dust and decay. But when you look very closely, you can still see the glory that it once possessed. Parts of the painting even appear in their pristine condition, though other parts clearly do not. More than that, you see what the painting could look like if it were to be properly restored. If an expert were to work with it, surely it could return to its intended state. I see no reason why God could not do the same with our world. The same applies to the bodies we currently possess. They still carry much of their glory, resembling the Creator who made them in His image and according to His likeness. Yet, they possess neither the gleam nor the resilience that they once had. Like our world, our bodies are in desperate need of an upgrade.

The Heavenly Man

There remains a substantial and lingering question here. If the end of our existence will bring about a new world, and we will live in a glorified creation, *how* exactly will we live? What will we look like? How will we act and behave? There are so many questions. Fortunately, God did not leave us without answers to these questions. We have a pattern to examine. More specifically, we have a *person* to examine. Most of us have heard a comparison of this sort before, and perhaps even many times before. Yeah, yeah . . . Jesus is who we should strive to copy and imitate . . . we are supposed to be like him . . . what would Jesus do? . . . etc., etc. This entire concept is something that can easily become cheap and cliché, but we can never allow that to happen. If we see the whole picture of what Jesus really means as our perfect "pattern," particularly with regards to the topics of this book, we can come away with an entirely new level of appreciation for what Christ has done in our world. More than that, we can see where we are going.

Early in the book, I went to great lengths to discuss the concept of what it means to be made in the "image" and "likeness" of God. Despite what Christian thinkers have read into the text over the last two thousand years, the biblical authors understood these concepts as having to do both with our nature *and* our physical bodies. If we simply allow the Bible to speak for itself—rather than inserting various philosophical and scientific perspectives into the ancient writings—we would have to come to such a conclusion. We must always remind ourselves that the single most significant question we can ask when trying to interpret the biblical texts is, what did the authors intend? The *authors*, not the readers. How did they comprehend and/or record the events we are reading about? There is much talk about viewing the Bible in its original context, but all of that magically vanishes when it doesn't say what we want (or need) it to. In this case, the writers did everything they could to portray the reality that Adam was made to resemble God in a comprehensive way; humanity was created to follow God's pattern. We were supposed to think, feel, love, imagine, will, and communicate like God. As I have argued throughout the book, we were even built to physically resemble God. None of this would of course involve an exact match. We were made to pattern God, not to be God.

When human disobedience led us away from the Creator's design for our lives, we lost aspects of the Image and the Likeness. In a powerful sense, the pattern was broken. The light dimmed a bit, and the color faded. Like the painting analogy from earlier, aspects of our existence still vividly mirror our Lord, while others only vaguely do (if at all). Clearly, something had to be done to restore the human portrait to its intended state. This renewal is part of the larger salvation narrative explained in Scripture but is unquestionably one of the most crucial elements. The restitution of humanity to the image of God and a return to the proper pattern involves many different aspects, but it fundamentally comes down to two things: an internal change and an external change. We must be transformed both *inwardly* and *outwardly*. The internal change in our nature comes about through God's Spirit working within us, and Jesus perfectly displayed what this type of life should look like. After doing so, he showed us what it looks like to be outwardly changed as well. But let's begin with the inside and work our way out.

To most outside of the church, Jesus was at least a wise man of epic renown. As a matter of objective fact, Jesus is the most famous person in human history, and it's not overly close. To those who believe in him, Jesus perfectly exemplified what human beings are supposed to be: how we should live our lives in a fallen world. I have often been asked the question—in one way or another—how do we know we are living the Christian life? One could respond in a multitude of ways, but most end up being overly weighty and almost always clunky. I feel that the easiest way to answer this question is to respond with one of my own: are you becoming more like Jesus, or more like Adam? I use the term "becoming" because holiness and the transformation of our inner nature is a process that does not happen overnight, nor is it ever fully accomplished. In my opinion, spiritual growth will not even cease after we are raised from the dead to live with Christ. The process continues, because life continues.

The question about becoming more like Jesus or Adam may seem overly simplistic, but it gets to the heart of the matter. The apostle Paul also believed this, and he used the comparison in the two ways I am proposing: as an example of both inward and outward change. The former appears in the book of Romans, which is easily one of the most theologically-driven writings we have from Paul. Throughout most of the first four chapters, Paul's mission was to ensure that every believer in Rome understood something very important: no one has merited salvation by their own doing. As Paul famously put it, "all have sinned and fall short of the glory of God" (Rom. 3:23). This was true of the Gentile believers and the Jewish Christians alike. This was invaluable information for that particular group, since Jew-Gentile relations in Rome were extremely strained at that time.[130] Having established that all people are equally in need of forgiveness, Paul further tightens the reins in chapter five. There, he reveals that Adam's actions led to a world in which we are "enemies of God" (Rom. 5:10). Though we once possessed a natural bond with our Creator, the Fall left us with a natural separation. In this, the human condition defaulted to being estranged from God. Put another way, we are all like Adam: not the Adam God intended, but the Adam who remained after his rebellion. Whereas being like Adam was once part of God's excellent Creation, it is now a badge of dishonor that guarantees our entry into condemnation. Paul clarifies the state of being that we all participate in: "Therefore, just as through one man sin entered into the world, and death through sin, and so death spread to all men, because all sinned" (5:12).

Regardless of our era, geographical location, age, gender, ethnicity, religion, political views, or anything else, every human being is born into "Adamdom." We all inherit a fallen condition (views vary on the extent) and an opposition to God. Death is the first result of this condition, and it is a certainty; ". . . it is appointed for men to die once and after this comes judgment" (Heb. 9:27). Left alone without a mighty work of God, this condition (and our own sinful deeds) would further lead to what the Bible calls the "second death" (Rev. 2:11, 21:8). This, of course, is what we commonly understand to be hell: everlasting punishment, Gehenna, and the lake of fire. The root cause of all this is Adam, and the influence Satan had upon him. It is a terribly ominous reality that far too few take seriously. Apart from some miraculous fix to the broken system, we would all be headed there.

---

[130] This friction came about after the Jewish people—some of whom had now accepted Christ—returned to Rome after Emperor Claudius had expelled them near A.D. 49. When they returned, battles over the role of the Jewish law and how the church should operate ensued. The result was somewhat of a religious elitism on both sides, particularly from the Jewish Christians.

Once he had them where they needed to be, Paul flipped the script on the believers in Rome, announcing that Adam is obsolete. Better said, Adam has been replaced. In a very real sense, Adam served as the progenitor and the prototype for all human beings that would live after him. As the first ever created human being, Adam held both a unique and powerful position. Some have referred to this role as the "federal head" of humanity. While some scholars squabble over whether this is accurate, it is unavoidably rational, and it makes sense of Scripture as a whole. We just considered Paul's words in Romans 5:12, for example. Besides this, denying the Fall altogether shifts the blame to the only other viable option: God. If we are not responsible for the world being out of sorts, then God must be. This would produce innumerable scriptural difficulties and would paint the portrait of a schizophrenic deity. God would despise human sinfulness but be the cause of it. He would hate evil but need it to exist. Most specifically, God would require Jesus to lay down his life for a problem He created. The entire biblical narrative would fall apart.

Keeping the story together, we are left with the consequences of Adam's sin. Not only does Adam's peculiar position mean that his life and decisions dictated the pattern for the rest of us, it also means that he determined our future. In order to fix the problem created by Adam's rebellion, it would be necessary to replace him as the federal head. However, that appears to be an impossible act. Since, logically speaking, there can only be one "first man" in history, how could we replace him? Wouldn't we have to go back in time, and put someone else in his position? Well, that would be one option (if it were possible). But there is another way it could be done. In fact, it has been done.

There is still a man that stands as the head of humanity. You see, Adam was merely "a pattern of the one to come" (5:14, NIV). Paul explained the situation as follows:

> "For if by the transgression of the one the many died, much more did the grace of God and the gift by the grace of the one Man, Jesus Christ, abound to the many . . . For if by the

transgression of the one, death reigned through the one, much more those who receive the abundance of grace and of the gift of righteousness will reign in life through the One, Jesus Christ. So then as through one transgression there resulted condemnation to all men, even so through one act of righteousness there resulted justification of life to all men. For as through the one man's disobedience the many were made sinners, even so through the obedience of the One the many will be made righteous" (5:15, 17-19).

The major concept at work here could not possibly be more important. The "one" man (Adam) brought a specific result, and the "One" man (Jesus) brought about the complete opposite result. Through his transgression, Adam brought about sin, condemnation and, ultimately, death. Through his perfect obedience, Jesus brought about righteousness, freedom, and everlasting life. The negative effects that came through Adam's demise were reversed and replaced through Jesus' triumph. Adam's pattern was broken by Jesus and, with its destruction, a new pattern emerged. Being forgiven and regenerated, we can now follow Christ's pattern.

If this is true, what do we see in the life and actions of the new Adam? In an overarching way, we see in Jesus humanity as it should be: humanity existing in the unblemished image of God. This manifested itself in numerous ways. Jesus was the one and only example of a sinless human life in all of history. In order to destroy the power of sin, he needed to be a completely unblemished sacrifice (1 Pet. 1:18-19). In Jesus, we also see someone who displayed what it means to truly love others. Beyond the obvious—but essential—fact that Jesus suffered and died for the very beings he created, we see this in many other ways. He forgave those whom others deemed unforgivable (Jn. 4:1-24). He ate and socialized with those whom others considered to be immoral castaways (Mt. 9:9-13). Jesus elevated the downtrodden, including women and the impoverished (Mk. 12:41-44). He even elevated children (Mt. 19:14, Lk. 17:2). On numerous occasions, he liberated people from demonic possession (Mt. 8:28-34, Lk. 4:31-37). He even healed multitudes of people from their afflictions, including some who simply touched his clothes (Mk. 5:25-34). The biblical examples I referenced for each of these barely scratch the surface. Jesus did these things (and many more) on a daily basis throughout his entire ministry. As the "beloved disciple" once said: "And there are also many other things which Jesus did, which if they were written in detail, I suppose that even the world itself would not contain the books that would be written" (Jn. 21:25).

When discussing all these aspects of Jesus' character, we all too often forget something else about him: he was perfectly just. This justness led him to physically expel those who had profaned his "father's house" (the temple), turning it into a cutthroat loan outfit (Mt. 21:12-13). At other times, he gave deserving individuals a tongue-lashing they were likely to never forget. The words "whitewashed tombs," "children of Satan," and "brood of vipers" come to mind.[131] Jesus was never shy about calling out hypocrisy, double-talk, and evil speech. In fact, he regularly went after his own disciples when they broke from his impeccable moral standards. Jesus famously gave one of his inner-circle apostles this shocking command, when Peter tried to persuade him to forego his necessary death: "Get behind me, Satan" (Mt. 16:23). While Jesus showed an incomparable concern for the contrite of heart, he also knocked the scoffers off their high horses whenever necessary. Of course, Jesus always knew exactly where each person stood, which enabled him to render these judgments correctly. He was also quick to caution others about unworthily making judgments of their own: "You hypocrite, first take the log out of your own eye, and then you will see clearly to take the speck out of your brother's eye" (Mt. 7:5). In Jesus, the world saw the complete character of God. Amazingly, we also saw this character in human form. All of this was done to show us the pattern.

Much more could be said about Jesus' exemplary life, but these examples provide valuable information about what it means to live as

---

[131] See Matthew 23:27, 23:33, and John 8:44, for some of Jesus' most blistering descriptions.

Jesus did. They also show us a great deal about what Adam's life was intended to be. This is the power of Christ's life: the Son of God took it upon himself to enter our created world as a mere mortal, so that he could show us what our lives can look like. More than that, he showed us what our lives *should* and ultimately *must* look like when the Kingdom comes in its fullness. It is right that the church has focused on the earth-shattering importance of Jesus' death, resurrection, and ascension. To be sure, these events changed the world and have allowed the unworthy (us) to be accepted into God's good company. But we cannot miss something equally important: the pattern Jesus left for us. Hopefully, this point has become clear.

These realities caused the apostle Paul to make the following declaration: "Therefore we do not lose heart. Though outwardly we are wasting away, yet inwardly we are being renewed day by day" (2 Cor. 4:16). Because of Christ's work, we can now be inwardly transformed and renewed into the image of God; that is, *right now* and *today*. Christ made this possible through his life, death, resurrection, and his institution of a new pattern of life. By his unique position as both God and man, Jesus replaced Adam. This inward work is accomplished through God's Spirit. With the Spirit's help, we can exhibit the personality and character that was intended for us. We can produce what Galatians describes as the "fruit of the Spirit:" love, joy, peace, patience, kindness, goodness, faithfulness, gentleness, and self-control (5:22-23). With this wonderful news, there is an important caveat to mention. While we can be now be inwardly transformed, the physical effects of being born into the image of Adam remain with us. There is still the outward issue to attend to. As you might have expected, God has already addressed to this problem as well.

The comparison between Jesus and Adam has another major function. In order to properly understand it, we will have to turn to a familiar place where Paul discussed the matter. I will not rehash the context of the situation that existed in Corinth, because I previously covered it in detail.[132] Despite the serious moral issues that were occurring, additional problems arose. One of these problems was that the church at Corinth had become infatuated with "spiritual things." Like the culture around them, they were obsessed with certain Greek philosophies, particularly the insistence that immaterial realities supersede material ones. As a side note, I have noted that the church has adopted much of this thinking throughout the last two millennia. In short, some within the church at Corinth had come to hope for a day when they would live as disembodied spirits. That was what they perceived to be the hope of the afterlife. To combat this mistaken ideology, Paul told them what the afterlife would *really* look like:

> "So also is the resurrection of the dead. It is sown a perishable body, it is raised an imperishable body; it is sown in dishonor, it is raised in glory; it is sown in weakness, it is raised in power; it is sown a natural body, it is raised a spiritual body. If there is a natural body, there is also a spiritual body. So also it is written, 'The first man, Adam, became a living soul.' The last Adam became a life-giving spirit. However, the spiritual is not first, but the natural; then the spiritual. The first man is from the earth, earthy; the second man is from heaven. As is the earthy, so also are those who are earthy; and as is the heavenly, so also are those who are heavenly. Just as we have borne the image of the earthy, we will also bear the image of the heavenly" (1 Cor. 15:42-49).

Paul could not have been more emphatic: the Christian hope for the afterlife is not to live as disembodied beings, but to live as fully embodied beings. Their hope in getting rid of physical existence was radically misguided and has no place in God's plans for us.

Obviously, this passage has similarities to what I previously discussed in Romans 5. This time, however, the comparison between Adam and Jesus

---

[132] Refer back to the section, "Points of Contact," for details about the church at Corinth.

is almost entirely about their physical, outward appearances. Paul even goes so far as to call Jesus the "last Adam," a title he only hinted at in Romans. This should alleviate any remaining concerns some may have about the notion of Jesus replacing Adam as humanity's prototype and pattern. Perhaps the most important thing to start with is Paul's statement in 15:44b: "If there is a natural body, there is also a spiritual body." For the Corinthians, this would have utterly flattened their obsession with discarding their bodies. However, it also shows that there are two primary types of bodies that exist among God's created beings. The first is the "natural body," which Adam possessed and we in turn possess. As Paul noted, the natural body is completely unfit to live on into eternity (15:50). As I have suggested, we all have what I would call "FBS." That is, Fallen Body Syndrome. Our bodies grow old, get sick, wear down, and will ultimately give way to death. That is the state of the natural body we inherit from Adam's fateful decision and its consequences. Though Jesus made it possible to be inwardly renewed, we will carry the natural body to our graves; death is still a certainty for each of us.

On the other hand, there is a completely different type of body that exists. This is the body with which Jesus rose from the dead, and still possesses. In contrast to the natural body, the "spiritual body" is imperishable, honorable, glorious and powerful (15:43). The spiritual body is made different, it functions different, and it even looks different. Whatever type of tangible makeup we are talking about, we can be certain that the spiritual body is most definitely not identical to the ones we currently have. We already know that it will not deteriorate and wear out. Paul made that much clear. For two primary reasons, we also know that it will not look exactly like our bodies. The first is that Paul clarified this matter in the same chapter:

> "All flesh is not the same flesh, but there is one flesh of men, and another flesh of beasts, and another flesh of birds, and another of fish. There are also heavenly bodies and earthly

bodies, but the glory of the heavenly is one, and the glory of the earthly is another" (1 Cor. 15:39-40).

Heavenly bodies and earthly bodies are not the same; they are not made of the same substance.

We also know that the spiritual body is unique from the natural body for another reason: we have examples to prove it. After Jesus was raised from the dead, he appeared to many of his closest followers and others in the area. As I previously discussed, his physical appearance was clearly not the determining factor for those who were able to recognize him.[133] Mary Magdalene did not initially identify Jesus (Jn. 20:15), nor did his closest apostles when he appeared to them (Jn. 21:4-8). In fact, the apostles had doubts about who he was from a physical perspective, even after they sat down right next to him (Jn. 21:12)![134] Likewise, the two disciples who made the seven-mile trip from Jerusalem to Emmaus with Jesus never realized it was him until they sat down for dinner (Lk. 24:13-35). Even when they did come to understand that they were in the presence of divinity, it was entirely because they recalled Jesus' style of blessing the meal (24:30-31). There are other examples that could be mentioned, but the bottom line is that Jesus unquestionably had somewhat of an altered appearance after the Resurrection.

While it was truly diverse in many respects, it was much the same in others. Though Jesus' appearance was not that of a normal man, it was not contrary to the human form. No one ran away shouting, "I just saw some type of weird creature in a white robe!" None of the biblical authors recorded that the resurrected Jesus now resembled some unknown species of space-dweller, or anything of the sort. Jesus looked like a

---

[133] This topic was covered in the section, "Heaven is a Realm," in chapter one.

[134] "Jesus said to them, 'Come and have breakfast.' None of the disciples dared ask him, 'Who are you?' They knew it was the Lord." The only possible reason John would have mentioned this is that doubts remained about who Jesus was. Even when looking right at him, they were not sure. However, their miraculous catch of fish proved that he was indeed the Lord, so no one "dared" to ask who he was.

transformed human being: different in some respects, but identical in others. All these realities directly parallel what has been discussed throughout the previous sections of this book. The angels that appeared to Lot were called "men" by those who came hunting for them (and also by Lot). Yet, these two mysterious figures had something about them that drew the attention of all the men in the entire city (Gen. 19:4). As I pointed out, angels (and even God!) are frequently described as men throughout the Bible; the connection between us and the heavenly beings is *that* strong. This also fits the entire portrayal of humanity being created a little lower than the angels (Heb. 2:7). We are not presently on their level, but we will be.

We were made in the image of God. Through Adam's transgression, this image became tarnished and in need of restoration. Jesus—who is the Son of God incarnate (made flesh)—was physically born into the image of Adam. This tells us something incredibly important. Jesus came to restore humanity to the image of God, *both* inwardly and outwardly. Jesus is God's act of reclaiming the pattern we were intended to follow, and the image we were intended to bear. Biblical scholar, Gordon Fee, powerfully explains what this means:

> "The one who as the Son of God bears the divine image is also the one who by virtue of his death and resurrection is now re-creating a people into that same image."[135]

What we find is that our higher brethren (the angels) also bear this image. They look much like us, yet they do not appear exactly like us. Even though Jesus had been changed after the Resurrection and did not look identical to the Jesus of old, he still looked much like a human being. Further, notice once more that Paul described the resurrection body as a "spiritual body." This hearkens back to the issue explored in chapter two ("Unseen Forces") about what it means to be "spirit" or "spiritual." Jesus walked, talked, ate, and was *physically* present amongst his followers after

---

[135] Gordon Fee, *Pauline Christology*, 515.

the Resurrection, and that is biblically undeniable. At the same time, it is said that Jesus' body is "spiritual" and that he even became a "life-giving spirit" (15:45). This is also undeniable. What else could be deduced except the reality that tangible embodiment and spiritual things are not opposites? I have even gone a step farther, consistently suggesting that they are, in fact, complementary concepts.

These truths become more incredible when we consider that Jesus said we will someday be like the angels: "When the dead rise, they will neither marry nor be given in marriage; they will be like the angels in heaven."[136] Certainly, the context of the situation is specifically about angelic relationships as compared to earthly ones. However, the context is also about the reality of the resurrection and what our mode of existence will be like; the questioning Sadducees rejected the afterlife in its totality. Based on the overall evidence available, being "like the angels" has a serious bodily component to it. I have already presented numerous examples of angelic visitations, pointing out that the angels looked strikingly human, but not *entirely* human. After the Resurrection, Jesus was described in just the same way. When we put the pieces together, we see our connection to both Jesus and the angels even more clearly. In our tarnished state of being, we hazily reflect the image of God and the image of the angels. In our restored state of being—which Jesus so perfectly displayed—we will accurately reflect both the image of God and the image of the angels. We will join the angelic beings, reflecting God's glory in unison.

At the beginning of this section, I noted that there is a much bigger picture involved with Jesus—who is our great pattern—than is typically taught. Most of us understand the inward results of Jesus' life, death, and resurrection. We understand the destruction of sin's power and the transformation that can (must!) take place in our lives. What we often miss is that Jesus also produced outward results. Jesus did not only show us how to live in the image of God: he provided a vivid glimpse at how

---

[136] Mark 12:25, NIV.

we will tangibly bear the Image. The Son of God became a man in the fallen image of Adam. After conquering the grave, Jesus rose and later returned to heaven in the restored image of man. By coming in Adam's physical pattern and becoming the "last Adam," he showed us all what humanity will—and was supposed to—be like. We will someday exist with the same type of spiritual body that Jesus showed us. As it turns out, this is also the way in which the angels reflect God's image. When we join God and the angels in the new heaven and new earth, we will all participate in the same Kingdom, and we will do so with the glorious bodies of that Kingdom; ". . . our physical bodies cannot inherit the Kingdom of God. These dying bodies cannot inherit what will last forever."[137] *These* bodies are not fit for eternity, but the resurrection body will undoubtedly be up to the task.

Spiritual Things

At the close of this book, I would like to outline some of the most important issues that have been discussed. To keep from disrupting the overall flow of this section, I want to begin with a theme that permeates nearly every aspect of the book: the influence that "immaterialism" has had within Christian theology. While many of the church's most celebrated thinkers—whom I have often discussed—are ready and willing to label others as "materialists," they have subscribed to a worldview that is at least as problematic, if not more so. Their infatuation with incorporating Greek philosophical concepts—particularly, but not limited to, the Platonic variety—into theology has commonly resulted in either the denial or the perversion of biblical concepts. Because of this synthesis, clear and straightforward scriptural perspectives are sometimes turned entirely upside down. The goal of the "spiritual cognoscenti" is to ensure that anything physical is ultimately viewed as being inferior to immaterial

---

[137] 1 Corinthians 15:50, NLT.

realities. Whether or not it is always the intention, such a worldview suggests to us that nothing is what it seems. Most unfortunately, they have been quite successful in their efforts.

This is evident almost everywhere we may choose to look. While the Bible emphatically shows us that we were made in God's image, it is almost universally taught that this has nothing to do with the way we look. While both God and the angels consistently appear with bodies throughout the Bible, we are told that neither *really* possess them. Though Jesus rose from the grave with a transformed body—a "spiritual body"—some have suggested that he left it behind when he returned to heaven.[138] Though we can clearly read that Jesus and the angels ate with certain privileged human beings, some scholars have informed us that it was nothing more than a show. Though our world is tangible, we are told that we should reach for a world that is not. Though we have physical bodies, we are asked to believe that the goal is to live apart from them. Though the Bible tells us that the resurrection is the great expectation of the Christian faith, we are supposed to focus on immaterial realms for the dead. Even though the new heaven and new earth will be tangible realities, we are supposed to yearn for immaterial existence. The list could go on and on. I must wonder: what have we accomplished with all our "deep thinking"? Historically, philosophy and biblical theology have been viewed as two paths toward the same truth. Whenever these paths have diverged, however, philosophy won.

With that issue serving as the backdrop, we can look at some of the other important aspects of the book. The first is that the Bible describes not just one world or realm, but multiple. While heaven is regularly equated with the sky, this is not an absolute connection. By this, I mean that both are strongly associated but are seldom equivalent. Scripture provides numerous images of heavenly beings who live "above us," like God's throne being in heaven and His footstool being the earth (Is. 66:1).

---

[138] Please refer to chapter two's section, "The Rise of Immaterialism," to examine this claim.

Jesus floated into the sky and disappeared at the Ascension (Acts 1:9), and the Spirit descended from the sky at Jesus' baptism (Lk. 3:22). These events or descriptions are no doubt true but tell only part of the story.

We also know that Jesus appeared and disappeared at will, and that angels are said to have done the same throughout the Bible. Demons possess or influence certain individuals without being seen. In fact, the heavenly beings (including those who have fallen) are typically not seen. The apostle Paul explained this perfectly in Ephesians 6:12:

> "For our struggle is not against flesh and blood, but against the rulers, against the powers, against the world forces of this darkness, against the spiritual forces of wickedness in the heavenly places."

The biblical allusions to heaven existing in the sky in part come from the language used within Scripture, but also because heavenly beings are often seen coming from the sky. It is crucial to note that, in the Bible, any affiliation with the sky designates a power beyond human understanding. This may be the strongest connection that exists between heaven and the sky. With this being said, the "heavenly places" is a reference not to outer space but to a realm that surpasses ours. This realm lies over top of, and certainly exists alongside of, the earthly realm. While the heavenly beings can travel between the realms, we—in our current state—are unable to do so. When you think about it, the existence of multiple realms (or dimensions, if you'd rather) is the only view that can truly make sense of how God and the angels are described within the Bible, as well as how they interact with us.

The next two issues are bound together in significant ways. One of the most important questions in all biblical studies—and certainly in reality—concerns what it means to be made in the image of God. As I stated, the church has almost universally accepted that bearing God's image has *only* to do with our inner qualities. The matter is cast exclusively in terms of cognitive ability, personality, freedom, creativity, relationships, and other similar factors. To one degree or another, these are all valid considerations. However, we have missed out on one of the central parts of what it means to bear God's image: the physical part. While the biblical authors consistently made this connection, those who "know better" have always been here to tell us differently. In the first chapter of the book, I specifically showed that the terminology used to describe our closeness with the Creator most definitely includes a physical element.

It should be telling that both the Hebrew and Greek words for "image" and "likeness" typically entail a tangible association.[139] This is evident within the creation of idols throughout the OT, which were fashioned to look like the false gods they worshipped (2 Chr. 23:17). It is also evident in things like the altars that were built to emulate those from other nations (2 Ki. 16:10-16), and the furnishings that God's people constructed (2 Chr. 4:3). Just as humanity was said to have been made both in the image and the likeness of God, Genesis 5:3 tells us that Adam had a son (Seth) *in his own likeness* and in *his own image*. There, Seth was compared to Adam with the very same descriptive language that was earlier used to compare Adam with God. Colossians 1:15 even tells us that Jesus is the "image of the invisible God." Surely, this was not intended to mean that Jesus was loosely or somewhat similar to God. Rather, it was intended to express the closest of all image-bearing language; in Jesus, we were seeing the invisible God! We should certainly understand that being made in God's image entails myriad concepts, with some of them having nothing to do with appearances. At the same time, we cannot deny that appearances factor into the equation in important ways.

By extension, the notion that heavenly beings are incorporeal, unembodied, immaterial, or are in any way non-physical, should be vanquished from our theological perspectives. This simply isn't how the Bible describes them. There are no examples to reference where an angel appeared to anyone as an unembodied entity or without tangible qualities.

---

[139] I Refer you to chapter one, and the section titled "Lost Images." There, I describe these terms in detail.

In fact, the similarities between the angels and us are so prevalent that they are often described as being human! This occurred repeatedly, with Lot's heavenly visitors (Gen. 19:5-12) and the "young man" at the tomb (Mk. 16:5) being only a couple of the available examples. This directly corresponds with the teaching that we were made "a little lower than the angels" (Heb. 2:7), and that—after the resurrection—we may actually sit ahead of them (1 Cor. 6:3)! Even the Son of God appeared in the OT in physical form, later became incarnate (made flesh) in the man Jesus, and then rose from the dead with a transformed body. On top of this, there are multiple occasions where both the angels and the *resurrected* Jesus ate among us.[140] Anyone who wants to make the case that the heavenly beings are incorporeal will have their work cut out for them. Worse, they will have to assume that the biblical authors were either ignorant or misinformed.

While many other topics would be worth revisiting, there is one more that I want to specifically mention: where all this is heading. In no uncertain terms, the ultimate hope of the Christian faith is two-fold: the resurrection and the reception of spiritual bodies, and the creation of the new heaven and earth. Though the church has focused heavily upon the belief that we will go to heaven as disembodied spirits, the Bible *at best* provides very little reason to believe this. As I discussed, it actually provides an abundance of reasons to reject the idea. God has something in store for us that far surpasses such a reality; we get to exist with glorified bodies, the likes of which the heavenly beings possess. Additionally, we will also get to live with them in a world without separation. Though we currently have limited access to God and the angels, in the new creation we will live face to face with them. This is the greatest connection with the heavenly realm and its inhabitants that we could ever envision. The two great realms will someday merge to become one. This is the world that we are heading towards, and we could ask for nothing more.

---

[140] See the "The Jesus Diet," in chapter two.

These are a just a few of the many issues I addressed throughout this book. However, the overarching theme is that we may all be in need of rethinking some of our beliefs. Perhaps even *a lot* of our beliefs. The dichotomy that has, throughout the last couple millennia, come to exist between physical and spiritual things is false; it is an unnecessary firewall that simply doesn't mesh with what God has revealed to us in Scripture or reality. The lens of faulty philosophy has contributed most to this problem, as the Bible has far too often been taken to describe an ideal state of existence that is almost entirely different from ours. Chiefly, the "ideal state" would be in no way physical. Some of the church's prominent thinkers have been more than eager to hitch their wagons to this runaway beast. All the while, God has clearly revealed through his prophets, apostles, writers and ultimately, His Son, that tangible existence is not the exception to the rule. To the contrary, tangible existence *is the rule*. From our world, to the angelic visitors, to Jesus' resurrection body, to our future bodies, to the new heaven and new earth, this should be apparent. But instead of accepting what has been revealed to us, we have often turned every one of these ideas on their heads. We have chosen to embrace false perspectives, despite the evidence to the contrary.

The good news is that this way of thinking does not have to be our *modus operandi* ("mode of operating"). If we allow ourselves the liberty to let go—even a little—of what most of us have been told is "hard fact" and biblical certainty, we might just catch a glimpse of something amazing: something *heavenly,* even. Spiritual things are much more than an escape from the physical world. In fact, they are nothing of the sort. Being "spiritual" is not about shedding our bodies, departing from tangible existence, or even praying to an unembodied deity. Spiritual things are the things of everyday life. They are ingrained into the created order, if we are willing to see them. Spiritual things are food, drink, bodies, worship, people, worldviews, and anything else that can be elevated to reach the heavenly world of God and His angels. And that is precisely the point: everything we deem to be ordinary can be transformed into the extraordinary. As the Bible describes reality, this is what God is in the business of doing. God transforms the natural into the supernatural, the secular into the sacred, and the worldly into the spiritual. This applies to our hearts and minds, our bodies, and even the world we inhabit. We can place our faith in these truths, for Jesus told us exactly what to expect: "Behold, I am making all things new."

I want to offer my sincerest thanks to every person who found this book to be worthy of their time and reflection. If this is true for you, I humbly ask that you consider leaving a short review of this book so that others might have access to your thoughts on the topics I have presented.

Thank you, and God bless.

References

Aquinas, Thomas. "Commentary on John 21."
http://dhspriory.org/thomas/John21.htm

Aquinas, Thomas. *The Summa Theologica, 1:51:2*. Christian Classics
Ethereal Library.
http://www.ccel.org/a/aquinas/summa/FP/FP051.html

Barclay, William, *The Letters to the Corinthians*. The Westminster John
Knox Press. Louisville, KY. 1975. Print.

Bender, Bryan. "U.S. Navy drafting new guidelines for reporting
UFOs." Politico. April 23, 2019.
https://www.politico.com/story/2019/04/23/us-navy-
guidelines-reporting-ufos-1375290

Borchert, G.L. "Gnosticism." Evangelical Dictionary of Biblical
Theolog y. Ed. Walter A. Elwell. Grand Rapids, MI: Baker,
1996. N. pag. Print.

Bruce, F.F. Strong's 1504, "eikõn." BibleHub.
http://biblehub.com/greek/1504.htm

Calvin, John. "Tracts & Letters – Psychopannychia." Godrules.net,
n.d. Web. 15 Dec. 2014.

Chaffey, Tim. "Theophanies in the Old Testament." Answers in
Genesis. Jan 13, 2012. https://answersingenesis.org/jesus-
christ/incarnation/theophanies-in-the-old-testament/

Chapman, Michael W. "Global Study: Atheists in Decline, Only 1.8%
of World Population by 2020." CNS News. July 24, 2013.
https://www.cnsnews.com/news/article/global-study-
atheists-decline-only-18-world-population-2020

D.J.A Clines, "Tyndale Bulletin 19" (53-103). Tyndale Old Testament
Lecture 1967, Tyndale Bulletin 19 (1968) 53-103.

Clossen, David. "What does it mean to be made in God's image?" The Ethics and Religious Liberty Commission of the Southern Baptist Tradition. May 4, 2006. https://erlc.com/resource-library/articles/what-does-it-mean-to-be-made-in-gods-image

Craig, William L. "A Review of Paul Helm's Eternal God". Reasonablefaith.org. https://www.reasonablefaith.org/writings/scholarly-writings/divine-eternity/a-review-of-paul-helms-eternal-god/

Craig, William L. "Divine Simplicity." ReasonableFaith.org. Jun 1, 2009. https://www.reasonablefaith.org/question-answer/probability-of-fine-tuning/divine-simplicity

Craig, William L. "Is the Notion of an Unembodied Mind Defensible?" ReasonableFiath.org. https://www.reasonablefaith.org/videos/short-videos/is-the-notion-of-an-unembodied-mind-defensible/

Craig, William L. "Is the Cause of the Universe an Uncaused, Personal Creator of the Universe, who sans the Universe Is Beginningless, Changeless, Immaterial, Timeless, Spaceless, and Enormously Powerful"? ReasonableFaith.org. Web. 10 Oct. 2010. http://www.reasonablefaith.org/is-the-cause-of-the-universe-an-uncaused-personal-creator-of-the-universe

Craig, William L. "Jesus' Body." Reasonablefaith.org. Mar 09, 2009 https://www.reasonablefaith.org/writings/question-answer/jesus-body

Crenshaw, James L. Old Testament Wisdom: An Introduction. Atlanta, GA: John Knox Press, 1973.

Duchesne-Guillemin, Jacques. "Zoroastrianism." Encyclopaedia Britan-nica. https://www.britannica.com/topic/Zoroastrianism

Enuma Elish: Epic of Creation. L.W. King Translator. http://www.sacred-texts.com/ane/enuma.htm

"Estimated Totals for the Entire 20th Century." Necrometrics. http://necrometrics.com/all20c.htm

"Facts and Statistics About Infidelity." Truth About Deception. https://www.truthaboutdeception.com/cheating-and-infidelity/stats-about-infidelity.html

Fee, Gordon D. *Pauline Christology: An Exegetical-Theological Study.* Hendrickson Publishers. Peabody, MA. 2007. Print.

Griffin, Carl W., Paulsen, David L. "Augustine and the Corporeality of God." Harvard Theological Review, Vol. 95, No. 1, January, 2002.

Griffin, Carl W., Paulsen, David L., "Simpliciores, Eruditi, and the Noetic Form of God: Pre-Nicene Christology Revisited." Harvard Theological Review, Vol. 108, No. 2, April, 2015.

Gottstein, Alon Goshen. "The Body as Image of God in Rabbinic Literature." Harvard Theological Review, 87. 1994. https://www.cambridge.org/core/journals/harvard-theological-review/article/body-as-image-of-god-in-rabbinic-literature/854AF4883B0464149B26D107679643C6

Irenaeus, Against Heresies. http://www.newadvent.org/fathers/0103506.htm

Kaiser, Walter C. "Jesus in the Old Testament." Gordon Conwell Contact Magazine. 2009. http://www.gordonconwell.edu/resources/Jesus-in-the-Old-Testament.cfm

Kean, Leslie. *UFOs: Generals, Pilots, and Government Officials Go on the Record.* Harmony Books. New York, NY. 2010.

Kent, H.A., Jr. "Paradise." Evangelical Dictionary of Biblical Theology. Ed. Walter

A. Elwell. Grand Rapids, MI: Baker, 1996.

Kugler, Mary. "The Joseph Merrick Story: The Elephant Man's Bones Reveal Mystery." VeryWellHealth. Oct. 18, 2018.

https://www.verywellhealth.com/the-elephant-mans-bones-reveal-mystery-2860454

Leisola, Matti. *Heretic: One Scientist's Journey from Darwin to Design.* Discovery Institute Press. Seattle, WA. 2018. Print.

Luibhéid, Colm. John Cassian: Conferences. Paulist Press. New York, NY. 1985.

"Maimonides" 13 Principles of Jewish Faith." http://web.oru.edu/current_students/class_pages/grtheo/m mankins/drbyhmpg_files/GBIB766RabbLit/Chapter9Maim onides13Princ/index.html

Merriam-Webster, "spirit." https://www.merriam-webster.com/dictionary/spirit

Merriam-Webster, "materialism." https://www.merriam-webster.com/dictionary/materialism

Middleton, Richard J. *The Liberating Image: the Imago Dei in Genesis 1.* Grand Rapids, MI: Brazos Press. 2001, print.

"Mythical Beasts: Blood for the Snake God." S1E5. https://www.sciencechannel.com/tv-shows/mythical-beasts/

Nelson, William O. "Is the LDS View of God Consistent with the Bible?" LDS.org. https://www.lds.org/ensign/1987/07/is-the-lds-view-of-god-consistent-with-the-bible?lang=eng&_r=1)

Origen, De Principiis. Christian Classics Ethereal Library. http://www.ccel.org/ccel/schaff/anf04.vi.v.ii.i.html

Orr, James. "God, Image Of." International Standard Bible Encyclopedia. http://www.biblestudytools.com/encyclopedias/isbe/god-image-of.html

Paulsen, David L. "Early Christian Belief in a Corporeal Deity: Origen and Augustine as Reluctant Witnesses." Harvard Theological Review, Vol. 83, No. 2, April 1990, pp. 105-116.

Paulsen, David L. *Early Christian Belief in an Embodied God: Part II* "Pneuma." BYU Studies Quarterly. Article 4, Volume 35, Issue 5. 1995. https://pdfs.semanticscholar.org/5ce5/3283c437a2af704fa47 07e063be08f258328.pdf

Piper, John. "Why Does God Regret and Repent in the Bible?" *Desiring God – Ask Pastor John.* May 28, 2017. https://www.youtube.com/watch?time_continue=480&v=g E0au-O3qM4

Polkinghorne, John. *Belief in God in an Age of Science.* New Haven: Yale University Press, 1998. Print.

"Quetzalcoatl." Encyclopedia.com. https://www.encyclopedia.com/people/history/mesoameric an-indigenous-peoples-biographies/quetzalcoatl

Rammel,E.C. "Pangu and the Chinese Creation." Story- http://www.ancient-origins.net/human-origins- folklore/pangu-and-chinese-creation-myth-00347

Rossiter, Wayne D. *Shadow of Oz: Theistic Evolution and the Absent God.* Pickwick Publications. Eugene, OR. 2015. Print.

"Ruach." Strong's Exhaustive Concordance. https://biblehub.com/hebrew/7308.htm

Scaruffi, Piero. "Wars and Casualties of the 20th and 21st Centuries." https://www.scaruffi.com/politics/massacre.html

Schaeffer, Francis A. Pollution and the Death of Man: The Christian View of Ecology. Hodder Christian paperbacks. London, England. 1970, Print.

Sherwood, Harriet. "Attendance at Church of England's Sunday services falls again." The Guardian. Nov 14, 2018.

https://www.theguardian.com/world/2018/nov/14/attendance-church-of-england-sunday-services-falls-again

Snyder, Christopher. "Did the story of Noah really happen?" Fox News. Mar 28, 2014. http://www.foxnews.com/science/2014/03/28/did-story-noah-really-happen.html

Strong's Greek Concordance. "epouranios". 2032. https://www.biblehub.com/greek/2032.htm.

"Suicide Rates in the United States Continue to Increase." CDC. NCHS Data Brief, June 2018. https://www.cdc.gov/nchs/products/databriefs/db309.htm

"Sumerian Myth." http://faculty.gvsu.edu/websterm/SumerianMyth.htm

Sunshine, Glenn. *The Image of God.* Every Square Inch Publishing. 2013.

Tertullian. Against Praxeas. http://www.newadvent.org/fathers/0317.htm

"The Confessions of Saint Augustine." Christian Classics Ethereal Library. https://www.ccel.org/ccel/augustine/confess.viii.i.html#viii.i-p0.2

"The Epic of Gilgamesh." Tablet 1. *AncientTexts.* http://www.ancienttexts.org/library/mesopotamian/gilgamesh/tab1.htm

Trench, Richard Chenevix. Strong's 1504, "eikṓn." BibleHub. http://biblehub.com/greek/1504.htm

Von Däniken, Erich. *Evidence of the Gods: A Visual Tour of Alien Influence in the Ancient World.* Career Press. Pompton Plains, NJ. 2013. Print.

Wallace, J. Warner. "Why Did God Create Angelic Beings?" Cold-Case Christianity. June 6, 2014. http://coldcasechristianity.com/2014/why-did-god-create-angelic-beings/

Weir, Kirsten. "Is Pornography Addictive?" American Psychological Association. Apr 2014, Vol. 4, No. 4. https://www.apa.org/monitor/2014/04/pornography

Whitmarsh, Tim. *Battling the Gods: Atheism in the Ancient World*. Knopf Doubleday Publishing. New York, NY. 2016, print.

Wright, N.T. "Heaven is Not Our Home." Christianity Today. Mar. 24, 2008. https://www.christianitytoday.com/ct/2008/april/heaven-is-not-our-home.html

Zuckerman, Phil. "How Many Atheists Are There? Hundreds of millions." Psychology Today. Oct 20, 2015. https://www.psychologytoday.com/us/blog/the-secular-life/201510/how-many-atheists-are-there

CPSIA information can be obtained
at www.ICGtesting.com
Printed in the USA
LVHW080619291019
635546LV00002B/799/P